ARRIVAL PRESS

BRASS TACKS

Edited

By

TRUDI RAMM

Hope you find this interesting

Phee

some really good poems in here.

lots of love

Bred

5th 4th Nov. 94

First published in Great Britain in 1994 by
ARRIVAL PRESS
1 - 2 Wainman Road, Woodston,
Peterborough, PE2 7BU

Foreword

A down-to-earth approach to life becomes increasingly desirable in these complicated times - even politicians are using phrases like back to basics and getting down to brass tacks to get their point across.

In this anthology a wide range of poets convey their feelings about coming to the point, cutting the waffle and speaking clearly in their verse. Some take a political standpoint while others convey the desire for simpler and more direct communication.

Robert Kenchington
Assistant Editor

CONTENTS

TRANSIENCE

Time in its own impatient way
Makes every month seem but a day,
And every hour like minutes tend
To bring us nearer to the end,
So if a lifetimes all we have
Live for each second - and be glad.

Mary W Priddey

BACK TO BASICS

Basically speaking we should drink more tea,
that's what back to basics means to me.
Go and put the kettle on, don't forget to warm the pot,
the state the country's in, no wonder we're suffering from shock!

Sue Koert

READ HIM HIS RIGHTS

You have the right to remain silent.
As the grave.
Ashes to ashes.
You have the right to the remains.
Such as they are.
Dust to dust.
You have the right to wrong.
Dubious honour.
Ashes or dust.

Nick Wilde

BACK TO BASICS

What's it all about. Why are we here.
Is it all chaos, doubt and fear.
Back to basics; let's be brave.
Set new goals, make time our slave.
Thrive on challenge, risk and change;
Soon success will not seem strange.

Paul Corrigan

REASON

I need to write
I need to think
I need the sight
To be able to blink
I need to ignore what I have thought
Don't need to look for what I have sought
I need a reason for being alive
I have to forget
I need to survive

Cathianne Hall

UNTITLED

Faith and reason held joint away
Long ago, but now today
Are politically defined,
Divorced, corrected, undermined.
Before a final Decree Nisi
State the churches should be busy
Reconciling in one vision
Education and religion.

Victor Green

JUST BASIC

Back to basics is just a laugh
It's how I am when in the bath.
Washed and scrubbed, I'm what I seem
Very basic and squeaky clean.
It's nice to think that in this way
I can be basic every day!

Marion Green

MISSING PERSONS

Where have all the people gone
From shops, offices and banks
Who, when I held the door for them
Once smiled and said 'Oh, thanks!'

Elizabeth Smith

POLITICS

They'd have us back to basics,
this government I'm sure.
Back to the days when the poor fought
to keep the bailiffs from the door.
When little boys as young as eight
were sent to mine the coal,
or up to clean the chimneys
climbing up the big black holes.
When if you earned no money
and your hovel rent was late,
you'd find yourself with your bundle,
standing at the workhouse gates.

Hazel Jones

BACK TO BASICS

It's essentially fundamental to recognise what is good,
  It's essentially fundamental to behave as we know we should;
If only veneers - well layered, and heavily lacquered with time -
  Could be stripped! We'd be back to basics . . .
But, would life be divinely sublime?

Kay Ennals

PEACE TALK

Sons of Ireland gird your swords
And let the magic of your tongues
Seek the path of peace.

The gift of the Blamey in your speech
And the wish for peace in this land
Shall melt hard hearts of man.

Mothers weep, and fathers dread the morn
While little children's hearts are torn
Let's give peace a chance.

Margery Wilson

BACK TO BASICS

Back to families,
Back to faithful love,
Back to prayer,
Back to church,
Back to the Bible
Back to God.

Judith Bedlow

BACK TO BASICS

B efore the recession,
A man said to me that the
C onservatives were great. Now he wants to
K ill them.

T he taxes are high,
O r is the pay low?

B efore the recession,
A ll the middle classes were happy.
S ad that they are not now.
I s this the
C onservative dream?
S hame.

Dave Briggs

FIRST THINGS FIRST

Whenever my life gets in a mess,
bringing problems thick and fast
Which way to turn, I cannot think
What to do first, or leave to the last.

Then, I go back to basics
It has never failed me yet
I do those things which *have* to be done
Things I must *not* forget.

Eventually, order emerges,
Everything irons out,
Once I've remembered *First Things First*
That's what it's all about.

F M Dixon

LOVE

Love is a
basic need
for us
as babies
and even
in later years
We seek it in
many forms
and places
We seek it in
noisy clubs
and pubs
music blaring
fit to deafen us - or
in the arms of
a husband
Finally we look
within ourselves
to find it
We hope it's there.

J R Pietrusiak

BACK TO BASICS

Back to back street abortions,
Back to poverty,
Back to hypocrisy,
Back to hardship,
Back to censorship,
Back to the Establishment,
Back to Basics.

Christopher Bedlow

BACK TO BASICS

You cannot put the clocks back
or wave a magic wand
But it really is quite simple
for the likes of you and me.

To keep the ten commandments
and to try to do good turns
And to think of others, as well as yourselves
the happier we should be.

This may sound dull on paper
but if your conscience is clear
You can then go out and enjoy yourselves
with no-one to interfere.

Irene Clegg

BACK TO BASICS

Have we wandered from the basics?
Has our culture lost its way?
Do we worship strange new idols,
Crowned with gold, whose feet are clay?

We shall need to do some thinking,
Conscience searching, painful slow.
No-one's perfect, that's for certain.
All have sinned; this truth we know.

Thankfully we have a Saviour,
One who died our souls to win;
Pointing us to God our Father. . .
In His strength we can begin.

June Chantry

BACK TWO BASICS

Scisab, scisab is basics backwards twice,
Say it again and I've said it thrice.
Why anyone would wish to *Back two basics,*
Sounds to me unbelievable tactics.
Back them to win, you'll be led a merry dance,
Back them each way (Basics scisab) could stand a chance.
Whether running the flat or flying over the sticks,
It's never really wise, to gamble on basics.
Einstein equation or formula used in the lab,
Will never equate, back to scisab, scisab.
Stay with experience, tried and tested practice,
When things go wrong, then go back to basics.

Dave Allberry

VACANT SMILES

I bounded to the crimson light for sweet
amusement; in through bright and lewd displays
of naked harlots posed to shame the day.
Where females lay in slumber at my feet,
Like mountain peaks their bosoms to defeat
with games through dark nights 'til it's time to pay!
The coldness in their eyes did shine no ray
of joy or hope; their missions not complete.
My gropes had made no change to hearts of stone,
Yet sadness peeped through eyes that gaped at me,
And though I went with rampant sexual needs,
I sensed they stood alone; this, their home,
For they were trapped inside pornography,
As pimps made loot through slaves in fancy beads.

Denise Russell

BACK TO BASICS

Begin by finding the key.
Then the answer you will see.

Start at the bottom, the roots.
Later you will see the shoots.

Simplify the difficult.
You will come to the result.

Elementary, Watson dear.
The answer is always near.

Think of it basically.
Get back to the primary.

Polly Bennison

AUTUMN THOUGHTS

Deep, golden bronze days,
Misty, silver idealic morns,
Dew laden early twilight,
Copper coloured russet leaves.

Laughing children scuffling leaves
The glowing harvest gleaned,
Fields full of stubble
Soon to be turned.

Early morning frosty haw,
Bracing breezes gently blow.
The bugle softly sounded
To me, this autumn mine.

S L Staples

PRIORITIES

Today I heard a woman
Talking about her pet rabbit
Explaining why she had paid
Several hundred pounds
On dental treatment, adding
That it was money well spent.

Today a television advert
Had a juicy lump of fish
On a bone china plate,
Garnished with a sprig of parsley
Delicately placed on a thick rug
For a pampered cat.

Today a bloated bag
Of hanging flesh and wasted bones
Sits in the dirt and dust
Human, hungry and homeless:
Only the buzz of flies
Disturbs the silence.

Richard Stewart

GOING BACK TO MY ROOTS

Back to basics, exactly what does that mean
Do we have to get our drinking water from the local stream
Do we have to go to work on a bike
Or better still use our legs and hike
Throw the WP out of the window, pen and ink was always best
Though it might make office work a lot slower I guess
There is one thing I would love to see
Thrown as far away as it could be
With it out of the way we could talk one to one
If we could just get rid of those damn mobile phones.

Melanie M Burgess

POLITICIAN'S CRY

'Back to basics' the politicians cry
Yet society continues to die
A slow, lingering death.

In order to heal
Humanity must reveal
What lies hidden at man's core.

Begin again from scratch,
Lift the latch
On morality imprisoned

Beneath society's infected crust.
Greed, violence, hatred, lust
But a few germ ladened jailers.

Young generations can no longer afford
Christian principles to be ignored
If promises of a future are to be fulfilled.

Julia Cutting

THOROUGHLY MODERN ME

What tangled webs of lies and deceit
We weave for ourselves, turn victory to defeat.
A web so small ensnares so great a fly,
Thus we find ourselves fettered, and eternally wonder why.
For we are bound by the limits of convention,
Are taught that certain things demand attention.
For money, power, possessions, success,
Are what we must strive for, with all the rest.
There is one thing that convention does not condone,
Living out our lives on love alone.

Vanessa Rivington

THE DIGNITY OF THE INDIVIDUAL

Independence of spirit is precious to me.
In others, of equal importance as in myself.
Performing life's duties with respect for
The individual
Is to reach the true stature of humanity.
To do what is right,
Without titillation of emotion - love or hate.
To react with caring, to foe as well as friend,
Is the ultimate
Dignity of oneself and another preserved.
Strive, though vulnerable, for the highest standard.
Hold fast
Though most travel another easier way.

Patricia Bourne

TO A NEW-BORN SON

Little one, what do your blurred eyes see
Still misty from the placental sea?
With miniature hands you finger the shawl
It doesn't feel like your mother at all.
Slowly turning your downy head
You search the shadows from your tiny bed,
The world is such an awesome place
But comfort is in your mother's face.
So hush, don't cry bewildered one
You are her joy, her love, her son.

Jill Willens

BACK TO BASICS IN EDUCATION

Back to basics means to me
Youngsters learning thoroughly.
For each child has a basic need
To learn their letters - and to read.
There's no short cut to number work
Learning tables cannot be shirked.
Calculators - the *in thing* today!
Simple - but fingers can go astray.
Learning by *rote* just has to be
The sure way to learn, for fluency.
I'm *not* against progress; computers; TV
But basically, it seems to me,
That a five year old with no alphabet
Is hardly ready for the mechanical set,
For advanced knowledge without basic foundation
Will *not* make us leaders in education.

Elizabeth Robertson

TRULY BLUE

The scandals that are coming out
About those Tory bores
The sex, intrigues, the deviants
That decency abhors.
We should be wary when we vote
Just who will make the Laws
Or it might become compulsory. . .
To sleep with pimps and whores!
So it's back to basics for them all
Get on the straight and narrow
And let them do what they were taught
At Eton or at Harrow!

Harold Hyman

ODE TO BACK TO BASICS

Oh tell me, Sir, what does it mean
This talk of Back to Basic's theme
Does it mean that you and me
Go back to Eighteen Thirty Three
Or is this thing Basic Instinct
Some awful tale no-one will print
This Back to Basic's theme of life
Would, Sir, explain it to my wife
We country folk of lowly breed
All know what can be grown from seed
And if this Back to Basic's be
Should we relearn 'bout bird and bee
And if this theme should cause a stir
Would you be kind and tell me, Sir
For Back to Basic's we all pull
Your sure it's not a load of bull.

William Arthur Littleford

BACK TO BASICS

When I first heard this phrase on the *telly* I thought, *what can this mean?*

So I went and got the dictionary to see what I could glean,
Having found the simple word *basic*, I still wasn't very wise,
So I sat back in my armchair and tightly closed my eyes.

What did this phrase conjure up for me? I wondered if I could recall.
For some reason it took me back in years to when I was very small.
The basics then were being honest and truthful and helpful and kind.
These were the things my parents had instilled into my mind.

Hazel Wild

A MATTER OF PREFERENCE

I walk along the shore beside
The magic waters deep and wide,
Where city people stop and say:
'There's nought to do here, let's not stay.'

The noisy mini-skirted minds
Of city folk, the stillness blinds,
For here there are but mountain streams
To play sweet music to one's dreams.

Mary Hayworth

DIFFERENCES

Why are they looking at me,
because of differences, granny?
'Just smile at them, my dear.
People are people - they're curious.'
So a little girl smiles her way
towards strangers.
Then stops.
On some faces there is no place
for kindness.
I won't offer
my smile anymore, granny.
I will wrap it nicely
and give it to you
as a birthday present.
And you, stranger?
Find it funny?
Still aiming to ignore
a girl
whose Down's syndrome
lets her down too?

Krystyna Lejk

THE CHILDREN

They have a right to be safe
the innocents entering here
Instead the world betrays them
filling us and them with fear.

I would dig a moat around them
erect ramparts ten feet or more
Shelter them from the outside
and crimson the keeper's door.

What have we done to the children
to those who are placed in our trust
We have failed in our duty to guard them
in a world that is no longer just.

Sandra Lindsay

BACK TO BASICS

Going back to basics isn't what I'd like to do
It conjures up some memories that make me feel quite blue.
The copper in the kitchen, the oilstove in the loo.
Freezing cold in winter with toes and fingers blue.
No hot water system, pipes just froze and burst
Cleaning up with chilblains on your fingers was a curse.

I think that I'll resist the old temptation to go back
Although so many things have changed, there's little that we lack
To make our lives much easier and help us on our way
Basically I'd rather stay the way we are today.

Patricia MacKinlay

MY BED

As I lay there, counting sheep,
I soon get cosy, and fall asleep,
A long day's toil, and in I hop,
In summer, I lay on the top.

My bed, it is a friend to me,
Through thick and thin, it welcomes me.
I climb within it's soothing folds,
Around my body, it softly moulds.

My bed and I, have been together,
Through polyester, back to feather,
Once inside, and tucked up warm,
I pity the ducks, their feathers. . .gawn!

Joy Clark

BACK TO BASICS

What? Give up my washer, my *micro* and cleaner!
Eat fatty meat, when I've got used to it leaner!
Give up my fridge and freezer of course;
Convenience foods *out;* cook meals from source?
No telly, CD, cassette or video,
Just back to listening to *Auntie* on Radio;
No electric blanket, or central heating. . .
(This way of life, some say *takes some beating!)*
Cars for the masses? No! Walk or bike;
Smog from coal fires; is this what we'd like?
We can't put the clock back; who'd want to try?
But *get back to basics* the politicians cry.
In this *technical* age our *children* must choose,
Look forward (or backwards) win or loose?

H M Birch

RETURN TO BASICS

The basics of my faith mean all to me,
To know that Jesus loves me as I am
And that He died for me upon that tree:
The eternal God, the sacrificial lamb
Who chose to die to cancel all my sin
To blot it from God's memory evermore
That life abundant in me might begin,
Continuing beyond life's earthly shore
Before the glory of the Father's Throne,
And in the presence of the ascended Lord,
Who rose triumphant from the grave to own
Those whom God's spirit touched through His true word.

Trust back to basics of the Christian way
In readiness for Christ's return one day.

Betty Stanley

DIGITAL DYNAMIC

Whenever you're feeling out of plumb
And deem your cerebrum's rum and dumb
From the hum of a life humdrum and glum,
A rule of thumb it has truly become
That, if on a table-top you drum
Your frisky fingertip and thumb -
Stunned by this fulsome fun-outcome,
Your mind starts singing to a strum
That triggers off wholesome wisdom
Within your quickened cranium!
Far less to tedium you'll succumb;
You'll see increase in your income -
For, stress your happiness won't benumb
And much boredom you'll overcome
If in drumming the digits you don't keep mum!

Pat Deighan

LAUGHTER

As I look through my window
I often heave a sigh
When I see the sad grim faces
Of the people passing by
Wherever is the laughter
That used to fill the skies
What's happened to the children
With smiling laughing eyes
Why does their sound of laughter
Seem so harsh and shrill
Could the reason really be
They're full of own self will
What's happened to the laughter
I'm sure we all once knew
Is it that we've really changed
Or just a phase we're passing through
Way back in my childhood days
When everything seemed sparse
Laughter came so easily
Life didn't seem a farce
Oh how I miss those good old times
When the whole world rang with laughter
Will I only hear that sound again
In the great Hereafter?

Iris Brown

SQUANDERED HERITAGE

We of vintaged years, so full
With essence of those years,
When even chance still there to take
And effort met with cheers.

All in all, a better life
Than that of youth to-date
For most, ahead is just a blank
For orphans of the state.

For them, adventure means the pub
To drive anothers car;
Unwanted numbers on the dole
They cannot travel far.

No longer Rule Britannia, or
Which uniform to wear,
The being posted overseas
For country that you care.

I would not change my gambled lot
With any youth abiding,
Confined within the British Isles
A land no chance providing.

Far better when the spirit strong
And substance flowed with ease,
When pride was order of the day
And foreign shores to tease.

When growing pains the open way
To stretch beyond the bounds,
Of this overcrowded island
Where hushed achievement sounds.

At least, we can remember
Better times now things are hard,
Unlike those who fill our space
But dealt the jokers card.

Henry J Green

LOVE IS THE ANSWER

We are going through a period in time,
When people seem to decline
From showing any emotion.
Hard as nails!
No sign of much devotion.
The old, the sick, the poor
Are a bore!
To this materialistic generation.
Money means more than devotion,
Yet most people have a sizeable portion.
Redistribution is what is needed
So the poor don't go short,
And we ease their burden.
The old, the sick, would be better by far,
If families were to take care of them more.
To care, to be kind, to live is the answer,
To follow the path of our *Lord* and master.

M A Threlfall

LIVING IN THE PAST

Back to basics means learning to live the way our parents lived.
Going back in time to the days of repression,
scrimping and scraping. Barely existing
living as they did during the depression.
Ever rising prices, the poll tax and mortgage increases
force us to pull in our belts which even now are tight.
The weak will suffer and quickly go under.
We must strive to go on, be aware of our plight.
The rich will get richer, the poor will get poorer,
the rest of us will be lucky to survive
as we struggle to exist on the merest pittance allowed.
Is this living? What a price we have to pay just to stay alive.

Dorothy Timney

MORNING DREAMS

I want to peel potatoes
Make my own bread
Pluck the goose
Use the feathers for my bed.

Keep chickens for their eggs
A goat for her milk
Friends I know
Think we're a joke.

Going back to basics
Is freedom to me
No stress,
Set times to eat my tea.

Home made wine, cheese
Having time to read.
Everyday
I satisfy my needs.

Back to basics
For some is sad
Try a little harder
It doesn't all have to be bad.

Emma Shaw

HAVE YOU HEARD THE LATEST. . .?

Why do we need to train these spies
And send them overseas?
It seems to me that usually
They get found out with ease.

Why do we need these radar screens
To monitor the foe?
If there's a use in such abuse
Then please pray tell me so.

Why do we need these satellites
That watch us night and day?
Where is the sense in this expense
When there's a better way.

We have on our side Mrs Jones
And time will surely show
If somebody starts World War Three
She'll be the first to know.

Paul Cecil

MAKING DO

By chance I've found a little book
it's very old and worn
It's full of hints and recipes
Presbyterian Church Loughmorne.

It's dated 1948
the price back then four bob
Proceeds for the heating fund
by those who worshipped God.

Rationing severe and hard
just after World War Two
Published and sold locally
to help housewives making do.

It sits up on my kitchen shelf
I look at it each day
Household hints for cooking
back to basics some might say.

A treasured book from long ago
no wonder it is worn
An inspiration it has been
from the ladies of Loughmorne.

Catherine Barrons

BACK TO BASICS

I retired years ago from the teaching profession,
what is the matter with education today?
With pupils illiterate, teachers want more pay,
Let's get back to the old-fashioned way.

I taught the three *R's*, an excellent basic,
They never failed to do the trick,
Children could read, write, do sums and spell,
Schooldays were happy for us and them as well.

Teachers criticised the new exam called *GCSE*,
when introduced into the Norfolk County.
Controversy arose over school history,
Pupils were given credit for skills rather than facts,
A teacher won the day ***Basics are to be brought back.***

Margery English

FORGOTTEN FRUIT

Do we think that we're wise,
We can now have the prize,
without the commitment of love?
I am not religious,
but if you claim to be,
this is not what is taught from above.

I am not old-fashioned.
I do believe in passion,
but our standards are all going wrong.
So let us return,
to how it should be,
and let's keep these things
where they belong.

Eve Chapman

GETTING IT RIGHT

When people gave you the time of day
When children could go out safely to play
When family life was part of our way
Where did we go wrong.

When simple things didn't cost much money
Like picnic treats, bread spread with honey
When skies were blue, days long and sunny
Where have they gone.

Times must change, that is part of life
Trying to improve the drudgery and strife
But streets are unsafe, crime is so rife
Where have we gone wrong.

What is the answer, what is the cure
Get back to basics, the ever open door
When people cared and you could be sure
That we had got it right.

Joyce Morris

BACK TO BASICS

Looking through glossy cook books galore,
hoping to find something for tea at four.
Find mouth-watering dishes I'd love to try,
but never got the ingredients, have I?

The preparation and cooking time
is usually long,
that is my *hour or two* gone!
So back to my old cook book,
that helps me each time,
to do just as nice recipes
for this family of mine.

Gwyneth John

BACK TO BASICS

Many years passed, so full of woe
Wondering then, which way to go
Worries a million worried me so
It's now that I've found how to let go
I became a healer, to help those in need
Worried, depressed, as I'd been, indeed
I think now I've found, the light in life
I'm no longer worried and full of strife
Back to the basics of how we should be
Learning to love and waiting to see
Clearly we start with love in our heart
For we must spread love, till we depart.

Hazel Bowman

ERADICATING CRIMES

How would you try to eradicate crimes
That cause so much suffering in these lawless times?
Would you tighten the laws to make punishment bite
In the hope that young people would then choose the right?
Or should the police concentrate on detection
And streamline procedures to record detentions?
Already much money is spent on alarms
To stop thieves and vandals from doing much harm.
The basic solution is to uplift our thoughts
Improve moral standards that children are taught,
Avoid entertainments that dwell upon vice,
Seek the alternatives - they should suffice.
When there's discipline and morals are high
Criminal tendencies should not arise.

Herbert Taylor

THE OTHER HALF

No home, no car, no phone,
These things all gone now I'm on my own,
I thought that it was just a divorce,
Surely there's another course.

Back to basics, nothing left,
Feeling empty and bereft,
You've taken things I worked hard for,
Not only alone now, but also poor.

My worldly goods no longer mine,
And here I am without a dime,
But at last you're no longer part of my life,
And I'm glad to say I'm no longer your wife.

Allison Magee

FORWARD IN THE 1990S

The priests and people had a plan.
Atop the list of things to do
Was *Spread the Word to ev'ry man*
And each young child and woman too.
We went right Back to Basics.

It should be easy nowadays.
Technology has many ploys
To broadcast far God's loving ways.
Effectively to share his joys
Should we go Back to Basics?

We listened silently in prayer
Till Wisdom spoke from ages past.
We heard the voice, became aware.
Give alms it said *and pray and fast.*
You must get Back to Basics.

Barbara Whitehead

WHY TODAY

Why is love replaced by hate
When peace should bring hope?

Why is food taken away
From those who starve
When we have so much for ourselves?

Why is one man poorer than the other
When wealth could be shared
To ease his burden?

Why do women fear their own back yards
When the streets
Should be safe to walk?

Why are humans caged
When freedom should be given?

Why is life taken so easily?

Is it because we have lost our sense of morality?
Or because we forgot to love each other?

Andrew Collins

BACK TO BASICS

Going back to basics,
Is a little phrase I'll never forget.
I remember when I was in school,
Where teachers made the simplest rules.

Sitting there in my maths class,
The teacher looked at my work and said, 'You'll never pass.'
I must admit my mind was numb,
She picked up my pen to show me the sum.
She said, 'You'll have to face it,
I'll have to take you back to basics.'

Gloria M Rees

BASIC CONCERNS

Why can't politicians ever answer a simple question?
I suppose it's because a yes or a no
Is beyond their comprehension.
They cloud the issues with which they're confronted
With long statements that avoid the facts,
Blaming somebody else for the things that have happened
Well there's nothing clever in that.
Half of them are too old for the job
And are living in the past,
So why do we vote them into power
When election promises never last?
It's gradually become a sad fact of life
That the people's opinions do not matter,
All they do is take our votes
Then our hopes and illusions shatter.
Okay then, let's get back to basics
Starting with the politicians in charge,
Let them set the good examples first
That can be followed by the people at large.
Let them try honesty, truth and good morals
And sack those that don't toe the line,
Only then will they earn the people's respect
And deserve your vote and mine.

Patricia Frampton

TEN OF THE BEST

Back to basics
That's the stuff
Of present ways
We've had enough.

Murder, rape
Battered wives
Child neglect
Ruined lives.

Muggings, theft
Vandalism
Joyriders and
Terrorism.

Sadly crime is
Ever growing
Prisons filled
To overflowing.

Back to basics
Good suggestion
Where to start
That's the question.

What is wrong
With rules well known
Writ long ago
On slabs of stone?

Dorothy M Hargreaves

BINGO GIRL

I wanted *Legs Eleven* when I caught a glimpse of Heaven
That looked about the number right for me.
Unaware of my regard, with her eyes down on the card,
To turn her head I couldn't find the key.

To make a good impression at any Bingo Session
I'd miss a *line* and never even moan.
If only I could tell her that here's a likely *fella*
Could help her get a *Full House* of our own!

H Jones

EXCUSE ME PLEASE

Why is everyone so rude
With such a belligerent attitude
I must admit that I was taught
Basic good manners will cost you nought
I hear some parents, shouting aloud
To very young children, when in a crowd
It makes me cringe, I find them shockers
Using words once only used by dockers
The elderly say the young show no respect
But by being observant, you can detect
The complainers really are just as bad
Refusing help rudely, when they should be glad
The butcher, the baker, whatever the trade
Forget serving us is the way money's made
No welcoming greeting, no time for a jest
It's *what do you want?* and you feel like a pest
With all the world's troubles, it may seem to you
The loss of good manners is trivial, it's true
But think what a much nicer world it could be
If we all stopped pushing for *Me Me Me!*

Frances Gregan

ANOTHER LIFE

Psychic power can touch us all,
By a feeling, sight or a call,
I believe it's a *God* sent gift,
Meant only to give us a lift,
For us to know there's another life,
Where there's no pain, worry or strife,
Sometimes these events can upset you, it's true,
But there's a reason for spirits coming to you,
Usually it's to warn or just to care,
So never be afraid when they're there.

L P Smith-Warren

1919 - SOME CHILDHOOD MEMORIES - 1924

Down Memory Lane, my thoughts return,
To the inn, where I was born.
The bedroom curtains, quivering there,
As the draught crept through at dawn.
A cloth lay on the window sill,
To soak up condensation.
Of what, did folk deny themselves,
To help the weary nation?

Spluttering logs, upon the hearth,
On an icy winter's day,
Small children, trudging thro' the snow
To school, three miles away.

I vividly remember now,
The *privvy,* way beyond.
'Twas quite a walk at night you know,
Especially past the pond!
So, what *do* folk complain about,
From January to December?
And awful lot, if, unlike me,
They are too young to remember.

Mary Peagram

VICTORIAN SPLENDOUR

Queen Victoria, sad, disheartened,
England going down the drain,
Gladstone's Bag, a shady lady,
Jack the Ripper strikes again.
Albert's Palace, crystal see-through,
South Sea bubble goes off *pop!*
Brunel's atmospheric railway,
Looses suction. Proper flop.

British Army, something lacking,
Fighting Zulu and the Boer,
Officers not quite real soldiers
When it comes to modern war.
Charlie Dickens, slums and sorrows,
Sherlock queries, 'What goes on?'
Watson, writing Sherlock's doings,
Wonders, 'Is he one big con.'

Dark satanic slums a 'spreading,
Breeding illness, rats and lice,
Public men, seeming clean living,
Forcing young girls into vice.
Church and chapel goers Sundays,
Crooks and perverts through the week,
Not all Victorian Splendour
If you care to search and seek.

Phil Wills

GOODBYE TO THE LOT

Goodbye to the Depot and clock card
Weigh-bridge and Lorries in the yard
Goodbye to Overalls and working Boots
Goodbye, Goodbye, who gives two Hoots?
They would have Gambled their weekly wage
that it would never reach such a stage
when they would be Presented with the News
that Private Contractors would handle the Refuse
And Dispose of them in one big Sweep
Those Bidders willing to do it Dirt cheap
Other towns and Cities are also Tightening the lid
Obliging those Contractors who make the Lowest Bid
Goodbye to the Sweepers who cleaned our Roads
and the loyal Dustmen who Emptied our rubbish in loads
When doing so 'twas always service with a smile
it didn't have to be Parcelled or wrapped in Tinfoil.

Francis Hughes

BACK TO BASICS

He saw the cottage on a bright spring day,
When all the hedges where white with May.
The sun shone softly on gambolling lambs
And the sky was blue as it arced the land.

His home in the town looked less appealing,
As he gazed at the oak beams that supported the ceiling.
He ignored the remarks by the owner clear,
That there's no electricity, gas or mains sewerage here.

Public transport too is long gone I fear,
But all of this fell on his very deaf ears.
He told our children he was to move their home
And was little alarmed at their barrage of moans.

For think he said they'll soon learn to like it
And without a doubt they'll become very bike fit.
Spring turned to Summer and the deal was done
And town was just left as winter had come.

It's snowing outside and the Aga won't light.
We're out of oil and it's as black as night.
The yard's full of mud and the streams full to bursting
And on top of that, there's even a worse thing.

He leaves at six with joy on his face,
Still muttering soliloquies of this heavenly place.
He returns to the town, to his central heating and buses
And quells all our moans with, I don't know what the fuss is.

While I learn to hold my breath, as I rod yards of septic piping.
The children all scream the snow's too deep to bike in.
I ignore my pungent odour and drive them to school
Back roads don't get cleared I'm afraid that's the rule.

Gone are my dreams of baking bread and tatting,
I'm far more likely to spend my time ratting.
So be warned my sisters you really must face it,
If you move to the country it's you who goes back to basics.

Val Miles

BACK TO THE STONE AGE

Back to basics,
What does the term mean?
To many people,
It is an outlandish government pipe-dream,
With little thought to the now,
Or the future unseen,
How basic does one have to become?
Back to cave dwelling,
Stone for weapons,
Hunting animals to eat,
Sketching cave walls for recreation,
No shoes on one's feet?
Privatise this, privatise that,
All commodities subject to Vat,
Policies seem so very crass,
Back to basics,
Will we win or lose?
Perhaps back to basics,
Is just another government ruse?

Shirley Boyson

BACK TO BASICS

Heavy snow fell overnight,
Next day our world was white.
The snow plough visited in the day,
Aiming at clearing a free way,
But milkman and postman never came,
They couldn't get down the lane.
Later we lost both phone and power.
Did it make the day turn sour?
Double glazers did not ring,
And the microwave ceased to ping.
Instead we revelled in the calm,
Dead machinery caused no harm.
We enjoyed a huge coal fire,
Watching flames reach ever higher,
Relaxing in the ruby glow,
Which warmed us all from head to toe.
The TV screen stayed dark and quiet,
No longer showing scenes of riot,
No longer intruding on our peace,
We wished the day would never cease.
And when day's light failed to beam,
Candlelight reigned supreme,
Casting soft shadows round us folk,
Who had the time to laugh and joke,
And talk and listen to each other,
No distractions, fuss or bother.

We often think about that day,
When we learnt to live a *different* way!

Nesta Wilson

FAIRY-TALE WORLD

Golden lands and ancient towns,
Fine castles fit for kings,
Enchanted realms of fairy folk;
So many wondrous things
Gave dream its bold dimension
In a war-whipped shaken world,
And flickered into embered nights
Where, in an armchair curled,
I sipped from legends of the days
When ogres roamed at will,
And heroes bent on chivalry
Made ready for the kill.
My hopes were pinned on beanstalks, then;
The real world I forsook -
Oh, would that I might dwell again
Within that story-book.

And would I were a child once more
Upon my father's knee,
That he might weave an endless store
Of magic made for me;
To find within a firelight's glow,
In all the moment brings,
That fairies roam enchanted lands,
And peasants can be kings.

Bernard M Jackson

BASICS!

'Back to Basics!' says the Leader,
So where do we begin?
Is it fundamentals
In a World engulfed in Sin?
        There are so many Basics
        On which we can build,
        But it is yet not clear
        How the footings should be filled!
Reading, writing, arithmetic,
Or Moral Cleansing, first?
Starting with the children
Those three Rs must be rehearsed!
        But from the Pinnacle of Society
        Should not some foundation be laid,
        Some cleansing from the ceiling downwards
        Then much Progress might be made!
Are those to whom we doff our hats,
Bow the head or flex the knee,
All worthy of such submission?
Do they behave better than we?
        The Backbone of the Nation,
        The trunk of the tree,
        Is the honest band of workers;
        Without them, where would we be?
There one finds the family,
Even when life is grim,
Standing firm together,
Faithful till eyes grow dim!
        Are we not victims of fake values,
        Blinded by what we see?
        Deceived by many in whom we trust,
        Oblivious to their hidden lust?

Claude Knight

THE WITNESS

In our solid first world homes, we
Have watched the flickering eyes,
In the last few moments of life.
We, who have witnessed this tragedy,
In the age of nuclear power, and
In glorious technicolor on our
TV screens, know not whether
They have gone to a better place.
But, we, who live, have witnessed,
And not only witnessed, but have
Allowed it to happen, as if, it
Was a natural phenomenon, like an
Eclipse of the moon, therefore we can
Do nothing about it, like an act of God!

To die within sight of the European
Sugar loaf mountains, to die of thirst
In a small boat in the middle of
An ocean. To die in a world,
Where there is neither first
World or third world, and we
Are all equal in the great hunger,
To die the pitying death, which engulfs
The whole world, when none shall witness
The event of TV in glorious technicolour,
When none shall know whether we have
Gone to a better place, or whether it
Is a natural phenomenon, like an eclipse
Of the moon, or an act of God!

Gerard Kenny

MAJOR'S MINERS

Day black dawning, cold frosty the morning,
Sad faced the miner, the pit wheel unturning;
All still, all quiet, all left to decay;
The mine and the miner here lived their last day,
And what will become of bread, roses and wine,
What will become of the miner, the mine?
No more will he go underground for coal,
His future will lie in the queue for the dole.
But what money can buy the pride and respect
Of the hard working miner sad left to reflect
On what will become of wine, roses and bread,
What will become of us now hope is dead?
What will become, as the government's hand
Squeezes the life from this hard working band?
Hear them all sigh all over the land,
Hear them all sigh; 'We don't understand.'
And what will become of the bread, wine and rose,
What will become of us? God alone knows.

Keith Tomey

SIMPLY BE

Oh why are the trees all lying down
could they not swim and therefore drowned
as the angry river through the valley ran,
no, it was the machine of man.

It saws and cuts and hacks and fells
a triumphant cry of *timber* it yells
as the angry sky sheds showers of tears
weeping unashamedly and expressing fears.

Fears for us the so-called intelligent race
man who is computerised and who has conquered space
through the angry river and weeping sky, the *way* we should see
Live in harmony with Nature. . . and simply be.

Jayne Singh

STARTING-POINT

What back to basics means to me,
is love and respect for the family.
But this has been lost as time's gone by,
just look around and you'll see why.
Times have changed but not for the best,
as parents work to keep up with the rest.
No time to stop and talk or play,
it's always another long working day.
A simpler life is needed now,
but high cost of living the question's how.
With children and teenagers the streets left to roam,
they really need their mothers at home.
But mothers are torn between the two,
and don't know what is best to do.
If they don't work there's no money to spare,
for trendy clothes the kids want to wear.
Oh mum we must have that they say,
so mum's off to work for another day.
The base of basics is plain to see,
it's a firm foundation for the family.

Sybil Smithson

THE BASIC BRITONS

I wonder if the Basic Britons
Were miserable all day,
And snapped at the children for nothing
And shot unnecessary prey?

Did they say, 'What terrible weather!
I can't see a thing in this murk;
If I'm not careful, I'll stumble
In the den where the boars lurk,

It's washing all my wode off,
It's running all over my skin.
We must have angered the sun-god,
We must have committed a sin,

We'll sacrifice something or other.
Come on, you over there.
That's it! I thought so:
There's now some light in the air,

Oh dear! It's started again.
We'd better all go to our beds.
Let's choose a corner that's dryish
And cover up our heads!'

Muriel P Knight

BACK TO BASICS

Back to basics, what does that mean?
In chambers dictionary I look.
There's several definitions,
But, *fundamental* is the one I took.

Fundamental? - Yes, I look for that
For enlightenment of the truth,
Basal - serves as groundwork.
I can only murmur *struth*.

So what do politicians mean
By this high and mighty phrase?
Do they just think up these sayings
To put us in a daze?

What must we all get back to?
Was the past so really great?
If it was, then, why oh why,
Have *they* led us to this state?

What grand examples have they set
To ennoble our young folk?
To some of these honourable persons
Honour in fact, is a joke.

Elsie Whipp

BACK TO BASICS

Ink and pen and rubber too
These few things are old not new
Count your blessings one by one
All your sorrows will be gone
Words of comfort love that's true
Whisper softly I love you
Take your partner by the hand
Hand to them a golden band
Send best wishes to a friend
Any quarrels you should mend
These few things if you would do
Bring rich blessings home to you
Give your children time of day
Teach them well learn them to play
These few things not meant in jest
Are heaven sent they mean the best.

K Twigg

BACK TO BASICS

Back to basics is all the single mother needs
staunch morality, upon that her child will not feed.
Suckling from a mother young in years and old in life
a scapegoat in pregnancy never to be a wife.
Her lover battered her and pushed her down with his heavy fists,
when all she wanted was a tender loving kiss
to heal the wounds.
She struggles on her own below the poverty level
in a damp infested one bedroom flat.
Back to basics forgotten are the vulnerable
look towards The Good Samaritan parable.
With eyes closed turn the other cheek
and be blinded to the needs of the weak.
It is written that the meek will inherit the earth
Christ in their salvation will clothe and feed each new birth.

Julie Mears

STATIONARY MOTION

The station called Birmingham New Street
Has steps to the various bays,
So I checked on the massive timetable
Then wandered about in a daze,
For I'd misread the sign to the platform
(My eyes must have been playing tricks)
So on reaching the end of the station
I had to *go back to Bay 6.*

Ken Miles

NEAR THE BORDER

I am old, but the sky is still as blue
As it was when all of my life was new.
I am old but I get the selfsame thrill
As I watch the moon trail its silver light
Through a wide clear sky on a quiet night,
When the world has paused, and the earth is still.

I am old, but the flowers smell as sweet
As in halcyon days, locked in love's retreat.
The heart lifts anew on a day of spring
When the bulbs first show through the wintry soil,
And fernfronds glow pink in each tender coil,
And I wait to see what the day will bring.

Time to remember the joys of the past,
Regretting, of course, that they could not last,
But enjoying today, with books to be read,
A crossword or two, a game of chess.
I am not afraid, as my days grow less,
To cross the border, and tiptoe ahead.

Jane Wilson

THE MESSAGE

Green grows the grass in our garden
  as it laps up the morning dew
How greedily it absorbs each raindrop
  that falls from out of the blue
I'm sure I can see it growing,
  the Daisies, gently waving, seem to say
It's too wet for you to get cracking,
  you can put the mower away,
A solitary bloom on the blood red Peony
  signals to all who would dare,
"Tis God's own wish, on a day like this,
  You'll the Grass and the Daisies spare.'

Bob Lawrence

BACK TO BASIC BASILDON

Back to basic Basildon some would like to be,
Where all values are so basic
Just like a cup of tea.
From the low life to the high life
Where some earn basic pay
We live in basic housing
Built on basic London clay.
We sign-on for basic benefits
To fulfil our basic needs
And our expectations
Are so very basically.

Basic Basildon could teach a thing or two
To Sussex or to Hampshire or even down in Looe,
We are a fine example
Of the Tory dream come true,
So it's back to basic Basildon
Our town that's all too blue.

Jenifer Akib

ALPHA AND OMEGA

Through the veil of space
From the realms of eternity,
Entire in his perfection,
Fresh from the arms of God
A child is born
And life's journey begun.

Slowly he travels
Through infancy and childhood,
His innocence lost in youth,
The lust for power
Enveloping his manhood
Speeding on the years.

Until the old man cries
'What profit greed and strife?'
All passions spent
He seeks his God once more
And glad in death
Is carried yet again -

Through the veil of space
To the realms of eternity
Redeemed and forgiven
Back in the arms of God
His soul has found
In Heaven its home.

Pearl Reynolds

BACK TO BASICS

What shall I buy for dinner?
Have we any bread?
Did I file that last report?
These thoughts whirl round my head.
Is someone collecting the children?
Do I need to go to the bank?
Have I filed that last report?
To be honest,
Now let's be frank.
Would it matter if I've forgotten?
Would the world end overnight?
Would anyone really notice?
No need to be uptight.
Try leaving it until tomorrow,
Lend each other some mutual support.
But in the back of my mind
Something's niggling.
Did I file that last report?

Susan Cave

WEEKEND FEVER

The supermarket was crammed, the wheels on the trolley wobbled,
Frantic folk all hustle and bustle, old people looking troubled.
Special offers to tempt us, on pork, beef and lamb,
No, I'll not be swayed from my egg and chips with spam!
My trolley is rebellious! Its direction is different to mine,
Now it's that corner shop I miss, no hurry and plenty of time,
What happened to that corner shop, we could *tick up* until pay-day?
Have a chat, listen to gossip, have a *fuddle*, pay a bit each Friday,
No worrying then about Xmas, or how we'd pay for that bird,
Now it's buy a turkey in September and freeze it! How absurd.
Today it's all hypermarkets, supermarkets, even cash-and-carry!
All rush and push, no time to talk, no time to tarry.
If I ever win the pools I'll open a real corner shop,
I'd sell packets of tea, small loaves, you can have one single chop!
My Xmas fuddle will be my pride, two bob a week all year round,
No stress as the season approaches of where the money will be found,
No trolley wheels to tap your heels and put you in a black mood,
Just a friendly atmosphere, make you welcome, and good food!
No piped music to distract, no cheese vacuum packed,
Dog biscuits in a sack, candles, nightlights, polish with real beeswax,
Bacon to slice as much or as little, fresh potted meat for tea,
Kettles that whistle, hot water bottles, and *Indian Brandy.*
My profit margins would be very small,
People, like you and me, are surely what counts after all?

Joyce M Hefti-Whitney

WHERE DID SUNDAY GO?

What happened to the seventh day, the day we used for rest,
Which marked the end of all our weekly toil?
Whose hand stole the Sabbath, that once belonged to God
And made the choice our quiet day to spoil?

Now the shops are open, like any other time
The tills ring out instead of sweet church bells,
Why did we throw away the chance of heavenly peace
And decide to venture to the shopping malls?

We used to picnic afternoons in the summer sun
Amid the unspoilt peace of country green,
Theatres now fling wide their doors to urge the public in
And try to lure them from the TV screen.

Where once the workers had Sunday to relax,
Now they return to do their daily job,
Sunday is forsaken for all who need to shop
And for the rest who want the extra bob.

Ann Rutherford

BACK TO BASICS

Nothing is for nothing
For all things there's a price
And man must pay
          The ultimate
   To enter Paradise.

Kent Gittoes

WHAT'S BASICS

There's going to be a terrible crush
At Basics.
Everyone is going to rush
To Basics.
It's not a law yet, but the cry has gone out
'To Basics.'
What will become of all the jets,
Computers and phones and TV sets
When people have gone
To Basics?
There'll be a demand - that's no surprise -
For space to breathe and to use your eyes
At Basics.
But what shall we do when nothing is new
At Basics?

Where will the teachers of ABC
And those who can count from 123
In Basics
Find minds that will learn more
Than ever before
In Basics?

Forget all your syntax, physics and maths,
It's Basics you need to stem all the greed
(That's basic!)
Yet men will be men as ever before
Without a new life and God's Spirit in them
To spark a desire from which would stem
Their return to true Basics.

Joyce Miles

GENTLEMEN

Kick back the mat; now do the splits; at last
I'm primed - ready to do a tricky pee
into a loo that's lower than my knee.
How many times I've missed and splashed right past.

The problem's with the *universal* pan
that's only universal if you sit
on it; but if you stand and aim at it
whilst full to brim. . . such are the trials of man.

It feels more natural to urinate
against something - secluded trees or walls
will do (with risk) to answer nature's calls,
but these are strictly for when one can't wait.

Now pubs know well what male problems can bring.
They know that gentlemen will flood the floor,
that's why they've come up with a simple cure:
provide ceramic walls with guttering.

John Cheetham

A STORM

Did you chose the men in grey
And find you have been led astray
By ready wit and silver tongue,
Leading where no song is sung. . .?

And do you listen as they preach -
Clapping at a pretty speech. . .?
But clever slogans that beguile
Only last a little while.

Is there someone you believe
Someone who will not deceive?
And will you still be on his side
If he has some sins to hide?

One man, with a simple phrase,
Urged us to reform our ways: -
'Back to basics, now!' he said -
And brought a storm about his head!

Joan Croft

DOWN REDCOAT

I remember in childhood, a winding walk
And fields where poppies grew.
The soft air filled with birds talk,
And sky of summer blue.

We set off down the *Lantern Hole*
Its real name Redcoat Lane;
And oh the joy of poppy fields,
Then home for tea again.

A toll was on the Halfpenny Bridge,
King buttercups grew wild,
Brown rabbits played along the ridge
The tiptoed breeze blew mild.

With nearby Kirkstall Abbey there
No journey since has seemed so grand;
A gently flowing River Aire,
And poppy carpet on the land.

To take that walk again today
Would break my heart in two,
To see the power station
In the fields where poppies grew.

Kathleen Rudd

WHAT'S NEW?

Have you read the story
about the days of old.
A tale of a girl called Alice,
and streets that were paved with gold.
Or a story about the high seas
and swashbuckling pirates, bold,
preying on stately galleons
filled with treasures and gold.
Maybe you've read the story
about the days of old,
when jobs were lost
and hard hearted landlords
threw tenants out into the cold.
Now it's not such a different story,
just like the days of old,
as the recession bites deeper,
and more and more businesses fold.
People wait in the dole queue
but their future has been sold.
Back to basics, well this is my view.
I think we're already there, don't you?

Mavis Fox

BACK TO BASICS

Back to building brighter future
For our children, not for greed.
Let past mistakes be our tutor,
Not destroying things we need.

Back to things that really matter,
Families, and cleaner air,
Not for fighting, have a natter,
For the needy really care.

Not afraid of getting fatter,
Set yourself another goal,
Not for all this slimming chatter,
Be yourself not half starved soul.

Back to reading, writing, spelling,
Arithmetic done in your head.
Now, computers do the telling,
But will they rule us instead?

Violet Croad

WITHOUT

Without a car we'd have to walk
Without a television we'd have to talk
Without a radio the world could not listen
Without a washing machine our clothes would not glisten
Without a newspaper what would we have to say
Without central heating the aged would freeze
Without front doors we'd have no need for keys
Without bricks we'd be back to using flint
Without supermarkets food would still cost a mint
Without ovens we'd still need fires
Without transport there'd be no need for tyres
Without baths we'd all be dirty
Without doctors we'd not live past thirty
Without aeroplanes we'd keep to the ground
Without rockets other planets couldn't be found
Without calculators sums our children could not add
Without most modern conveniences life would be so sad.

Cherry Somers-Dowell

BACK TO BASICS

I was busy ironing before getting tea,
I should have carried on.
A childish voice was calling me
'Mum listen to this bird with a lovely song.'

Piles of washing, veggies to be done,
time to put on the dinner.
'Please Mum come and watch us run
and see who is the winner.'

All these chores I left and more
for childish important things.
I have a happy memory store
although those years had wings.

So leave the chores they'll still get done,
if happiness you wish to reap.
Enjoy your children, share their fun.
Happy memories will be yours to keep.

Vicki Turner

TRAWLING THE DEEP

He lingers in the warmth
Of insulated hours
As the lights of Newlyn
Slip away:
Back to the swell
Of the open sea
And the slow passage
Of wind-torn days.

Running through the heat
Of an Atlantic storm,
Eyes like sewers
Mangled by sheets
Of boiling foam;
Then the silvery flow
Of beating gills
And sturdy nets

Bleeding pools of brine.
Back into the deep
For another trawl;
The cycle turns again,
And minds begin to hover
Beyond the horizon,
Scouring the mist each morning
For the watermark of home.

Alan Spencer

SUNBEAMS ON BLUEBELLS

Rising from the hot primordial slime
This limb reaches out, as mouth noise is shout;
This limb pulls over rocks, pulling for love -
Joined by the other, tugging for full care
While this limb kneels and prays that we should care.

Then the fourth stands, hold out the hands to give!

So, the back is straight and open eyes see daylight.
The joy at rising and walking away
But the feet should not ignore other's plight.
No-one should be downtrodden, open hands!
None be lost to drown in forgotten quicksands!
Sink not into that slime but live this day

With every man valued as a brother -
Sunbeams round bluebells, under canopy
Of forest like crystal streams forever!
Suzanne Stratful

THE WAY IT SHOULD BE

With more respect,
And more regard.
People more thoughtful, a little less hard,
Children as children, the way it should be,
Not trying to be adult, too quickly.
A lot more give,
And a little less take,
Not wanting things, for wanting sake,
Law and order, theme of the day.
If you do wrong, then you must pay,
A tightening up of all the rules,
A little more discipline, in the schools,
A lot less violence, would mean less pain.
And make a lovely world again,
Take the ten commandments as our guide,
And this country of ours,
  Will surely survive . . .

Jacqueline Claire Davies

TIMEWARP IN '39

I remember the time
in '39,
when the earth cast off
the pestilence of pollution
like the shedding of a cloak
that had become the bane of the world.

I remember the time
in '39,
when mankind ended
the atrocities of war,
and laid down their weapons
that had become an extension of themselves.

I remember that time
in '39,
when the earth regressed
to give one more chance
to imbue ourselves with higher values
and learn the lessons of unity.

I remember it well,
here in '79,
as I sit alone in my homespun den,
and ponder upon the passing of time,
and our return to the basics of life,
while the scavengers grovel outside.

Julia A Smith

THE RIVER FORTH

Dear old River flowing past these shores
Are you free from pollution and all the world's sores?
Or has the thoughtlessness and greed of man
Affected you too and invaded your span?
Is it not time, if not too late,
That conservationists take over the environment?
To save the earth, before others have sealed our fate!
Trying their best to amend all the wrongs that have been done
And we should support them, each and every one,
Making a better world for our children, and their children, to inherit,
So they can feel we are worthy of merit
Not a generation of power seekers
Having only self-interest and the greed for money in mind.
The world must halt! Think again!
Turn around! Start amending the wrongs
Leaving all the ills of the past behind!
May God protect your dear River and all your surrounds!

A Caring Senior Citizen

BACK TO BASICS

Back to basics what does it mean
What's basic what is not?

To me a roof above my head
A job to earn my daily bread,
A glowing fire on winter's nights
Through flickering flames
I'd set my sights,
On other comforts I could gleen
That for me a basic dream.

But others' basic needs are such
They don't ask for very much.

A cardboard box to spend the night
Someone to help them end their plight.
Where can they get their basic need,
A miracle or some good deed.
Like offer a home a job a meal
If it was you how would you feel.
Depressed dejected in despair
You know that governments don't care.

Their back to basics policy
To basic what?
Well you tell me.

Mary Jones

THE WAY FORWARD

'Back to Basics,' 'Back to Basics,'
Politicians cry,
'Back to Basics,' 'Back to Basics,'
'You say well,' say I,
But do any politicians
Mean just what they say?
Hardly ever, almost never,
That is not their way!

Back to Basics, Back to Basics!
What a good idea!
If all men would but pursue it,
(But they won't I fear).

Trust in God, and Love your neighbour,
Live an upright life,
Only gain by honest labour,
Husbands love your wife.
Wives respect and love your husbands,
Teach your children right and wrong,
Fill the home with love and kindness,
Help the young to grow up strong.

Let's be set for honest living,
Do our best at work or play,
Less for getting, more for giving,
Back to Basics, that's the way!

R L Grimwood

ANOTHER KIND OF FLOOD

No mercy shown for those who needed it
In this sad and barren land,
No sympathy or compassion
No help was close at hand,
Only the howling screaming mob
Crying out for blood;
Hatred, bitterness and intolerance
Drowning in another kind of flood.

How can we become so insensitive
Is this a sign of the times,
How can we search for reasons
When we don't understand the rhymes.
Man . . . who is born to woman
In the life-giving way
Disguised in the guise of human
In a flash can act this way.

Why don't we look into our hearts
If we dig deep we'll find the way
We were told, long ago, to love one another
There didn't seem much more to say.
What has happened to The Word
Has it been misunderstood
If we don't get together and turn the tide
We might drown in another kind of flood.

B McNally

BACK TO SCHOOL

Now, a grandmother thought she would go back to school
To brush up on her A, B, C.
She could never write things down very clear
And this bothered her you see.
Over the years she'd forgotten so much
The verbs, the nouns, the grammar and such.
Did she put a coma there, or maybe a full stop?
It's surprising to think she'd forgotten the lot.
Whenever she spelt words they never looked right
And her handwriting was such a terrible sight.
Now, how at her age should she really begin
Should she stop to think, or rush straight in?
Should she wait till next week before she will go?
It's a dreadful thing when your will power's low.
She swallowed her pride and took a deep breath,
Her knees started shaking it scared her to death.
All of this worrying wasn't much fun,
So she made up her mind what had to be done.
She purchased some books and some pencils as well
Then she started to write and learnt how to spell.
She learnt about paragraphs and wrote essays too.
It's surprising how much she's expected to do.
I wonder if she will become a great author
Who knows! We will just wait and see.
It's not easy to start at the very beginning
Especially for a grandma of three.

J Short

BACK TO BASICS

The code of life in former times,
Was very strict and formal,
So much so that people,
Couldn't call their lives quite normal.

Given too much liberation,
Things tilt the other way,
And too much pomp of yesteryear,
Is anarchy today.

Life is like a pair of scales,
And we can only try,
To get the balance of this right,
Or things just go awry.

So let's get back to basics,
Study things that once worked well,
Combine them with the best of now,
And maybe who can tell . . .

The world might be a better place,
For rich and poor alike,
So come on rulers of our lands,
And please get on your bike!

Mary E Hall

THEN AND NOW

How things have changed over the years,
Since the days that I was at school,
discipline then caused many a tear,
We dared not break the rules.

When I was a boy, I had to do,
The things that I was told,
Be on time, think it through,
Respect for those that were old.

Sometime later you'll have to go,
To work, and new things to learn,
When you start working then you'll know,
The satisfaction in what you earn.

Remember your elders have been around,
For many more years than you,
The skills they have are very sound,
So watch them and do what they do.

When you are older and take a wife,
You'll need to work for most of your life,
And a regular job with regular pay,
Will see you through for most of the way.

So stick at it then, apply common-sense,
In all that you do and say,
Cross the bridges, don't sit on the fence,
Life's not all work, there *is* time for play.

L G Domoney

BACK TO BASICS

You ask me what Back to Basics means to me?
It means going back to the way things used to be.
An open fire with cooking range and puddings in the pot.
Bread rising in the blackened hearth, muffins, piping hot,
Water on the boil, for a pot of fresh leaf tea.
These are some of the things Back to Basics means to me.

Families gathered round the table for a hearty meal,
All enjoying, laughing with that *togetherness* feel.
Neighbours popping in for a cuppa and a chat,
Open doors and open arms, a welcome on the mat.
Children skipping, spinning tops, playing with a ball,
Feelings of trust and love, for one and all.

If going Back to Basics makes the world a better place,
I know that it would put a smile on my face.
Life might have been hard in those good old days,
But surely life was happier in many different ways.
Everyone felt safer, everyone felt free.
If it was possible, *Back to Basics* is for me.

L A Griffiths

THE HAPPIEST DAYS?

What does *back to basics* mean
when I think of school?
Hands on heads, fingers on lips;
being beaten with a rule.
Mrs Brown, a gargantuan lady
who supervised our play,
dolling out sheets of toilet paper,
no more than four a day.
The lavatories were archaic,
a bacteriologist's dream.
A hut, a bench, a board, a hole,
flushed daily - 'twas obscene.

School lunches were a nightmare
one's plate must be wiped clean,
so lumpy bits were spat into hankies
and hidden where they'd not be seen.
Only ship's biscuits of bygone times
with weevils and maggoty meat
could rival our school salads
and the insects we had to eat.

I agree we grew up hardy;
learned that nothing in life is fair;
knew our tables backwards
anything less we wouldn't dare.
But if this is getting *back to basics*
it will not get my vote.
For I'll be heading out of here
by plane or train or boat.

Pauline Brennan

OVERFLOW

Scatter the blessing in their passing
As they come from day to day
In the giving and the loving
They will not decay nor fade away
Loving thoughts words and actions
Light the way to rise and soar
Scatter the blessing bounding raindrops
God provides there's more in store
There's a harvest in the making
Every day let it be known
Scatter the blessings in all our pathways
We shall reap what we have sown.

G Camp

WHEN WRITING A POEM

When writing a poem, my mind is like -
a cauldron of ideas from which up I will psyche
When a suitable subject that I have found;
The ideas for it in my head swirl round and round.

Once a subject has found seed in my head;
I reach for my note book before I lose thread
Because descriptive phrases and words will cascade
One line complete, with the other almost made.

To look up in the dictionary a meaning of a word
They often sound very absurd!
So onward my ideas flow freely forth
Joined in unison, hopefully, to produce a poem of some worth.

A task I do not ever recommend
I assure you, it will drive you round the bend
is to have inspiration, whilst in the bath you lay
The hot steam will dry up your pen, come what may!

Whatever the idea you have found
I am sure, soon, a story will abound
From a subject that has suddenly sprung from seed
Will flower into a poem for someone to read.

Sue White

INTERNAL REVERIE

Inside my head
is rubbish really.
Accumulated over my 28 years.
Old ideas, prejudices no doubt.
Angry words; words of praise.

Things I once believed in,
but no longer do -
old chestnuts jostling with
new concepts, struggling to gain ground.

How I cling to what I know
and fear to spring clean.
Time to dust off, sweep out
re-evaluate, and take on board
for a new century ahead.
So time for a new me.

Inside my head -
everything I will need
everything I won't
now's the time to decide.

Alyson Faye

BACK TO BASICS

I wish the Tories wouldn't make so much
of a very silly slogan that is such
an open invitation
to ridicule the nation -
the Germans wouldn't do it - nor the Dutch!

I really wish John Major wouldn't write
such poetry. (Please keep it out of sight).
A saying or a slogan,
(no, it needn't be from Wogan!)
could be written by a poet on the Right!

I really wish the Tories wouldn't sow
the seedlings of disaster as they go.
many feet on each banana
leaving problems for mañana -
Back to Basics means they fall before they grow!

British poets could do better, I am sure;
could, if asked come up with something that could lure
our condition from stagnation
with a bit of inspiration -
yes, I really think that poetry is the cure.
Estella St Clair

A,B,C - 1,2,3

After mastering the art of using your feet
Next comes the task of learning to speak
Followed by lessons of how to write and to spell
And then the introduction of numbers as well.

But it's easy you see, this ABC
Almost as simple as numbers 1, 2 and 3.
The alphabet whilst learnt by heart
Learning numbers is quite a different art.

So when you can't quite grasp these basic rules
You sit at the back of the class, in disgrace, the fool.
Then you may be tested in case you are deaf or just can't see
And no one can explain your illiteracy.

So you perhaps rebel a bit and drop behind
Because of a problem they cannot define.
Extra tuition or lessons are suggested
To counteract the dis-interested.

But still the letters look like BAC
And the numbers look like 2, 1, 3.
And so it's easy to be classed *defective*
Particularly when you are dyslexic.

G Ricketts

THE EARLY 1900'S

I was born in a small English village,
under a vast, encompassing sky.
Into a world of farms, estates, and gardens,
with poultry, pigs and sheep, and hungry herds.
The cottage tied, and *no place else* to shelter.

My kinfolk laboured daily through the seasons,
for basic needs, and sought no other ploy.
Their work, their God, did all their time consume.
Marriage bed and ale-house, their only respite,
kept cradles filled, and every family poor.

When sons and daughters wished in turn
to marry, and for approval brought their
sweethearts home. No fairness of face
nor form, concerned their elders, ability
to work, the only norm.

So I, a child with crippled feet, a burden was
deemed to be. National Health as yet unborn, higher
education nil, for a poor man's child. Though eager,
bright and intelligent, with needs quite plain to see.
No help could be found for such as me.

What changes in the village now. Fast car by cottage
door, help for the handicapped, National Health, and
education for all. Many moons have waxed and waned since
the day that I was born, in those frugal, hard, care-worn days.
In the early 1900's

M E Ireland

THE BEST OF BOTH WORLDS

Is *Back to basics* just what it seems,
If not, what does it really mean?
Perhaps then, we should all go back
To curlers, corsets, and bowler hats,
Unheated bedrooms and baths made of tin,
Outside toilets where the rain came in,
No hot water and far less to eat,
No extra money for leisure and treats.
Yet there was, I remember, a feeling now rare,
Of respect for the elderly, consideration and care.
Family closeness with father and mother,
Brothers and sisters who cared for each other,
Food that was tasty and often home grown,
Apples, carrots and greens in the garden were sown,
Drinking water was clean, and the air was still clear,
We could bask in the sun without any fear.
Our school days were shorter, we didn't have cars,
But all those that left school had mastered the *R's*.
Murder was rare, there was less petty crime,
We were safe on the streets whatever the time.
We knew more important than possessions and wealth
Was regard for each other, self respect, and good health.
So perhaps it is time to go back to the days
When we all helped each other in so many ways.

A E Janes

I DON'T WANT BASIC

Back to basics, what a lark.
I would rather be eaten by a shark.
We lived very basic when I was young.
When we had cake it was basic sponge.

Our house had only the barest furniture.
No carpets or even a nice picture.
Went for walks to avoid paying rent.
We didn't have the money. What we had was spent.

Did a moonlight flit to escape the bailiff.
Another bare room what a life.
Bread and jam great for tea.
Unless you get something given free.

No I don't want to be basic again.
To get away from it was hard work and pain.
So in my old age I feel more secure.
I would rather not be basic any more.

Dot Hewit

HAVE WE A BREACH TO FILL?

We've heard much of what has been said
  About their spelling and what kids have read
Or could not have done (or not really well)
  As too few of them know just how to spell!
And among those considered scholastic
  Some think spelling should be more elastic
Claiming written work's perfectly fair
  Whatever the spelling's like there
Leading to an absurdity (or so we have heard)
  That few understand even one single word.
And specialist teachers get somewhat obsessed
  About what they teach - forgetting the rest -
Like insisting on writing (to record what's been done)
  In a way that is clear and to just more than one.
Language is a lifeline we can never relinquish
  And one of the best in the world is our English
Whether spoken (or written) it should ever be
  Heard very clearly and (as clearly) to see.
So what's with our teachers and their country's weal?
  Should next generation be deprived of this *feel?*
So hoping teachers are not all that squeamish
  Keep teaching but teach 'em good English!

Wilfred Smith

BACK TO BASICS

I wake each morning and greet a new dawn
And wonder who today is going to mourn.
I switch on my radio for the latest news
Only to hear someone with very weird views.
How can a cruise costing five hundred quid
Change a delinquent, whatever he did?
A battered and bloody young girl is found
Raped and murdered and dumped on waste ground.
Back to Basics - what does it mean?
For some it's life that is drastically lean.
A cardboard box, can it be called home?
Hungry and cold and destined to roam.
These destitute humans are forced into crime
How can they live without penny or dime?
Murder and rape is all that we hear
It's no wonder people now live in fear.
Bring back the birch and cat-of-nine-tails
Hurt all those men who call themselves males.
Until a good deterrent is brought into use
Actions and morals will stay very loose.
Corporal Punishment should still be the law
Until re-instatement life will be raw.
The Good Book says, an eye or an eye
So why shouldn't all murderers die?
Members of Parliament, please take note
Next time it's raised - make the right vote.
If that young mutilated body is related to you
Surely you know the right thing to do.
Back to Basics just means for me
Ethical standards is what life should be.

Fran Lodwig

BACK TO BASICS

What does Mr Major mean
With his back to basics plan.
How far back are we to go
In the history of man
The Stone Age! I think not.
How about the sixties boom time
When jobs were in abundance
And we were doing fine.
Perhaps a swing to Labour
Would be a better scheme,
Could they stop computers replacing manpower
I think that is a pipe dream.
We've come so far so quickly,
Progress has become the fist
That grabs the money for the rich
With poor us way down the list.

So sorry Mr Major
I can't see this plan surviving.
I just hope we're not all victims
Of your parliamentary driving.

J M Jones

BACK TO BASICS

Men never grow up - I've heard it said
And as I look at the man on the bed
I can only agree 'How true, how true.'

A sergeant major in the Guards
The drill and war had made him hard
But he had seen it through.

Then back to home and family life
His children three and a patient wife
This man so strict they knew.

He led them through the daily storms
Of life, that took on many forms
As into age they grew.

But holiday habits die so hard
And here you see he drops his guard
And is a child again.

Mena Faulkner

BACK TO PREHISTORICS

According to many,
Man came from the ape,
Evolving from them,
Into a human-like shape.
Still very hairy,
And living in caves,
There were no Susan's or Harry's,
Or Margaret's or Dave's.
They had names like Ugg or Bog,
Iggle or Vigg,
And although not yet clever,
Their stomachs were big.
So they searched for food,
Some hunted *dinosaurs,*
Huge leafy-plant eaters,
Though some, *carnivores.*
And their favourite food,
Was a creature called man
Why they ate them?
I can't understand.
Man gave them indigestion,
So I'm convinced, without doubt,
That man was the reason,
Why dinosaurs died out.

Malcolm Penny

BACK TO BASICS

Back to nature a hole a cave
Wondering how the other folk lived
Imagine if it was you or me
Really climbing up a tree
Seeing if it was hot or cold
The weather clock so very old
Hunting animals just to live
Spearing fish a moment of glee
Aim is good we'll get our tea
Even the fire you go collect
Some sticks etc quite an event
Washing in a stream nearby
Really cold but we have to try
Okay when the sun is shining
Could stay in and paddle all day
But at night our caves they be
A haven for the family
But in this modem age we live in
Music blasting all the while
Would you change your mode of living
Makes one think and really smile
Thinking we have got it all
But long ago an era maybe
They just thought the same as we.

Sheila Macdonald

NOSTALGIA

Where has all the kindness gone,
That we knew yesterday?
When a simple *please* and *thank you,*
Was the *usual* thing to say.
Where are those friendly neighbours,
Who helped when things went wrong?
The interest shown - and *sympathy,*
To help each day along?
When everyone loved children
And still revered *the old:*
Their families used to care for them -
And saw they were not cold.
There always seemed *some time to spare,*
To lend a helping hand:
Before such *rush and hurry*
Obsessed our poor old land.
To us, who still remember, life's become
An *aberration.*
Our traditional British character,
Now gone - throughout the nation.
Our earth and sea polluted,
With man's revolting schemes:
Even the air above us, with monstrous
Missiles teems:
And God, is just another word - to use
When things annoy.
We, somehow, lost that *inner peace:*
That brought us so much joy.

Gaenor Spratley

BACK TO BASICS

So, *Back to Basics* Major says,
Back to all that's pure:
Revive the moral standards,
And, once revived, add more.

Teach the children right from wrong,
It's easy to explain.
The good they should aspire to,
From bad they must refrain.

How to achieve this backward step?
This idealistic course,
Find someone from our history
Who had a saintly force.

Perhaps it should be Robin Hood,
The poor did think him good,
The gentry, they felt differently,
But then again, they would!

The good and bad then basically
Should be easy to define,
We need to find a role model,
To whom we can align.

It's no good looking round us now,
Deceit and lies are rife:
No basic rules for them in power,
Ask any MP's wife!

And now we've set the record straight,
Put books away on't shelves,
Let's move *forward*, towards basics,
And define them for ourselves.

Ann Greaves

BACK TO BASICS

God made the world. He made you in it.
You have a need. God can fulfil it.
He gave ability. He gave choice -
So you can trust or reject His Voice. (Rev.4:11)
Life is a battle of Wrong and Right.
Independence of God, in His sight
Is Sin. We're created to go His Way -
Every moment of each single day. (Rom.3:23)
God's punishment for every *small* sin
Is *Death* -it's separation from Him.
Death is a place of *Time with no end*
Without the Love only God can send. (2Thess.1:8&9)
God is Love - all of which comes from Him.
He came to earth to pay for *your* Sin -
Died on a cross, then rose from the dead -
So you needn't die, but Live instead. (Rom.5:8)
Christ Jesus was not like you and me,
His sinless life was all purity -
So there was no way He could stay dead.
He rose, like cork in water, instead.
Christ conquered Death for you and for me
If we believe in His Divinity.
Christ Jesus died to pay for *your* Sin -
He'll give you Life if you trust in Him (1 Peter 1:3-7)
You have a choice, so what will you choose?
To accept or reject God's Good News?
You can't trust God yet reject His Son.
Will you believe in all that He's done?
Will you repent of all of your Sin -
Turn to Jesus, and trust only Him? (Jn.3:16-18, Rom.10:104 & 9-10)

J I Lord

PAUSE AWHILE

Pause awhile, and ponder -
Since Man was first conceived
In His mad pursuit of plunder
Little else has been achieved.
The time He spent conniving
To acquire ill-gotten gains
Wasted years of striving
With so little for His pains.

At first it was so simple
With a well-aimed hefty brick
'Gainst a victim, not so nimble,
It often did the trick.
Soon a barricade of boulders
In the entrance of a cave
Took more than brawny shoulders
And a tendency to rave.

The brick became a slingshot
The spear became a bow
And the victim now, as like as not
Was suddenly the foe.
If all that time and effort
In sowing seeds of war
Was spent, so that the young were taught
That only Love was Law.

If everyone gave freely
Of this His gift alone,
There'd be no word for poverty
Nor for the word Atone.

D E Vincent

BACK TO BASICS

What is happening in our world today
We are throwing all our pride away
The wheels of industry grind slowly to a halt
And the workers protest it is not our fault
Sure they have the right to the good things of life
To share with the woman they made their wife
Let us start again as we did in the past
And try not to expect success too fast
Father was the breadwinner and earned his pay
By putting in an honest eight hour day
Mother stayed home and looked after the child
And was able to watch it didn't run wild
War came along and took the husband away
The wife had to go to work and earn a pay
Came the end and the flag of peace was unfurled
No work for the men in this brave new world
So after all the poverty privation and pain
They started the war all over again
No time for the young men to learn a trade
But the second time round some fortunes were made
It was said we never had it so good
Yet a third of the world was starving for food
Again the gates are closing and the jobs are few
To all we old-timers this is nothing new
So what is everyone waiting and praying for
Heaven forbid that the answer is a nuclear war
Wake up all you men asking for an increase
Get on with the job and work for the peace
You were born by the union of man and wife
Thank God for every moment of this wonderful life.

G S Mutch

NEVER GIVE UP

I've decided to get back to basics,
To get on with my life, that's my plan.
I'll pick myself up from the ground,
Then dust myself off, once again.

Never give up, that's my motto.
Keep trying, for you never know when
The sun will start shining upon you,
And life will be happy again.

We all know that life isn't easy,
That at times it may cause a tear.
Just remember life is for living,
Look forward and be of good cheer.

We don't know what's round the corner,
But whatever it is, never fear
There's always a brand new tomorrow,
When after the storm, skies will clear.

Katina Pepper

HORSE-POWER!

Last night I heard the newsman say,
'Oil supplies grow short.'
We'll have to look for transport
Of a very different sort.

Horses are coming back again,
Already the signs are there,
Motorways soon may echo
The rhythm of carriage and pair.

Horse is still man's friend they say,
And so it will always be.
Am I mistaken, or can I hear,
The sound of an old man's glee?

My Grandad loved all horses
From the day that he was born,
He hated the scream of tyres,
The screech of a motor horn.

Clattering hooves on a cobbled street
Made music to his ears,
He grieved so at their fading
With many bitter tears.

If garages turn into stables
And cars with rust erode,
Will Grandad again come riding
Along some dusty road?

M E Beaumont

LOVE AND UNDERSTANDING?

It's easier not to check him when he screams and throws a fit
Of anger in a supermarket crowd,
Or smashes granny's antique plate (she was too fond of it) -
Correcting toddlers now is not allowed.

It's easier to press a switch and let him watch cartoons.
(I hated doing homework, years ago.)
Now everything's computerised he won't need boring maths,
And pictures tell him all he needs to know.

It's easier to go to bed. Of course he has a key.
He's only young and needs to have his fun.
It's no use preaching at him when he's growing up so fast.
He won't get into trouble. Not *my* son.

He's sitting in a police cell now. There must be some mistake.
It's said teenagers all love wheels. That's true.
But killing someone's child at speed, then burning up the car?
That's not the sort of thing *my* boy would do!

Audrey Forbes-Handley

FORWARD, BACK TO BASICS

Basics, may be old fashioned to the *in crowd,*
But that doesn't make them wrong,
Basics have lasted, for thousands of years,
Until the *in crowd* came along.

We were presented with ten basic rules,
Enough to build a Heaven on earth,
It may be *square,* to comply with them,
But that can never reduce their worth.

What can bring greater happiness,
Than a family, united and proud?
The love that stems from togetherness,
Starts at home, then reaches out to the crowd.

It's so easy to respect our elders,
But for them, where would we be?
They may not walk or talk so fast,
But thanks to them, our country's free.

When did we lose our honesty,
Why are windows and doors, all bolted tight?
Why must people live in fear,
Why are we so frightened of the night?

It all comes back to basics,
Those little rules, that all make sense,
The basics normally cost nothing,
So why do we perch, the couldn't care less fence?

We must move forward, back to basics,
Forget the *in crowd* ideas, they're incorrect,
Those ten rules must be re-established,
Before our heavenly earth is wrecked.

Dave Holmes

1940'S SCHOOL BASICS

Gymslips and navy blue knickers,
Liberty bodice and vest,
No easy-care, easy-wear nylon,
For cottons and woollens were best.

Gymslips and navy blue knickers,
A hard-wearing laced up shoe,
White hanky tucked up in your knickers,
And horrible dinners of stew.

Gymslips and navy blue knickers,
Beret and blazer and tie,
A satchel, so heavy, of leather,
And a look of respect in your eye.

Gymslips and navy blue knickers,
A gymslip was pleated, 'twas true,
But as soon as one sprouted a bosom
That gymslip did *nothing* for you.

Gymslips and navy blue knickers,
A one-piece for swimming, the rule,
When learning to dive one was seated,
Then lifted and thrown in the pool.

Gymslips and navy blue knickers,
Homework and books by the score,
That cane, a deterrent for cheating,
You never did cheat anymore.

Gymslips and navy blue knickers,
Games shorts that weren't very short,
White blouses of Aertex - and horror!
That end of the year, School Report.

Margaret Bradley

BASIC POLITICAL THOUGHTS

Pity poor John Major and his party
With the political debacle on view
Of *Back to Basics* - when the message seemed
To be *Do as I say, not as I do!*

Other politicians jumped on this bandwagon
When ministers' lives were laid bare
The whole issue was made totally political
But there's something of which we should all be aware.

Ignore the politics - the idea is good
Regardless of politicians' behaviour
And no party has all members whiter than white
So other Members of the House needn't jeer.

Surely we can think for ourselves
It doesn't take a degree
Or some highly paid Minister from either side
To work out what's best for you and me.

Basic human rights are important
Good education, skills and health
Humanitarian thoughts and values
This is our hidden wealth

We don't need a politician to tell us
What we already know
Too much greed and selfishness
Is our internal foe.

The only way forward I can see
Is to fight it from within
We should look at ourselves and make a change
And *Love thy neighbour* and care for him.

Joyce Siddle

THE BEGINNER'S GUIDE TO POKER

I'm a gambler from the Old Wild West
And poker is my game
It's a game of skill and if you lose
You've only yourself to blame.

I play stud and draw and bet my chips
Always hope for a winning hand
I might just bluff if it's not good enough
But I always make my stand.

Now I'll explain a bit about poker
You don't eat your chips they're not real
And an ace-in-the-hole is an ace face down
Toad-in-the-hole is an evening meal.

Five cards is a hand you put in your hand
You keep them close to your chest
You bet your chips which is a stake not a steak
Then you see whose hand is best.

To see you say *see* then you bet the same
To raise, raise the stake not your hand
At the end of the game everyone puts their hands down
To see where the pot will land.

Now the pot is the total of chips that's been bet
Not a substitute trophy or cup
So if that's not plain, more I will try and explain
Here's my card, when I'm in town look me up.

Then I'll tell you all about ante
This you bet before you begin
So there's ante and a pot and stake and chips
Good luck, I hope you win.

Keith Thornley

BACK TO BASICS

Back to basics to be exact,
is a phrase I'd like to base on fact.
Where have I heard these words before?
I seem to recall it's a government bore!

Back to basics - What can they mean?
To my mind's eye it's a government dream.
How can they justify what they say,
by the state of the country's wealth today.

We once had good times in the palm of our hand,
now government heads are buried in sand.
Jobless millions with no posts to seek,
have careers on hold with an outlook so bleak.

In caring professions a pittance is earned,
if the powers that be would only listen and learn.
Our dear senior citizens deserve certain rights,
they fought two world wars so we'd have peaceful nights.

We all search for hope and a future that's bright,
to be able to come home safely at night.
Our siblings' futures are in such dire straits,
we must strive for them - However long it takes.

Our homeland that was once full of hope and glory,
has been made to become a mere - Fairy Story!
If the powers that be would only push to the fore,
we'd again live to see a proud nation once more.

Val MacFadyen

BACK TO BASICS

Back to basics -
Base to apex -
Hardly know which way to face, ex-
Cept, with government's duplicity
Exposed by daily eccentricity,
We rather now would tend to question
If the Prime Minister knows best: yon
Profligate MPs indulge in knavery,
And Ministers attempt to say very
Clearly just what they mean
By *old-time standards,* when obscene
Books can be sold on Sunday,
But not the Bible on this one day.

Should researchers such as Gallup
Interview *Sun* readers, or a load of Trollope
Novel addicts whose IQ
Is based upon the likes of you,
Simply by questioning their writing habits,
And not if they have sex like rabbits?

MPs, strong men, whose status since election
We suppose would, in tradition,
Stand firm 'gainst provocation,
Be it fiscal, carnal, power-magnetized ambition;
And public trust, respect and rectitude be theirs.
Homo sum : humani nil a me alierum puto :
So Terence, long before the birth of Christ,
Consigned to us this day a truth not put to
One side as if insignificant,
But recognising that all men are oft enticed,
Enveigled, and at times recalcitrant.

Don Reeve

BACK TO BASICS

When bathnight came we had a tub
A tin one by the fire,
And one by one we took our turn
From smallest child to sire.

The copper heated all the day
The oil lamp gently glowed
While on the darkest winter night
We could see outside it snowed.

The black grate warmed and gleamed so bright
Nothing did we fear
E'en though with candle we would tread
Upon the stone cold stair.

Our cosy feather bedspread wrapped
Around our bedsocked feet,
With *rations* then our meals were sparse
Though we had enough to eat.

We dreamed of cakes and gooey sweets
And toys we could not have,
Then shuddering down with chattering teeth
We scurried to outside lav!

We walked to school a mile away
With chilblains on our feet
But weekends came and Sunday tea
We had our special treat.

Eight of us lived in a cottage small
We had such happy hours
If *Back to Basics* is the theme
Then this was surely ours!

Mollie D Earl

WORDS OF WISDOM

Growing into adulthood, we are often taught
To pick our P's and Q's
To do as we are told and not what we choose

We are told to be quiet and listen
Be seen and not heard
To go out in the big wide world, we are prepared

Go to your church every Sunday
Go to your school every day
Be polite in every way

Be patient and all will come
to those that shall wait
Always be early, never be late

Do unto others as you would have done unto you
Do not count your chickens before they hatch
If in doubt leave it out.

Early to bed, early to rise
they say
Makes you healthy, wealthy and wise

Sticks and stones won't break your bones
and idle talk is that of fools
Good, hard working hands are tools

Things are easier said than done
These things our elders teach
but what about my childhood, is that out of reach?

Yes, we can listen and do as we must
but let us learn from our own experiences
If in doubt, we'll learn without interferences.

Wisdom comes only from ageing
and that will come in time
but for now I'm growing up and this world is mine.

Lynn Skelton

PANTOMIME ON ICE

The rainbow came alive for me
last night, when I was there,
watching figures glide and skate,
shimmering shiny colours - everywhere.

Snow White sparkled as she sang,
dancing with the woodland life.
They protected her from wickedness,
stopping the hunter wielding his knife.

The magic mirror glistened silver
as she told the jealous Queen,
'Snow White is fairer still, than you.
In the woods she can be seen.'

A magic apple the Queen did brew
with the help of demons and rats.
The seven dwarf's cottage she soon found
through the knowledge of sinister bats.

Hi Ho! Hi Ho! The little men came,
hailing Snow White with a song.
The birds and the bees greeted them all
with the news - her life had gone.

Through all the show the pantomime horse
caused fun - and bursts of laughter.
He clumsily knelt to mourn the maid,
showing her off to his princely master.

Snow White awoke with the loving kiss.
The scheming witch was banished.
Wedding bells pealed over the ice.
The fairytale was ended, the panto finished.

Felicity Minifie

BACK TO BASICS

Back to Basics - let us walk in the park
It doesn't matter if it's light or dark
No need to look over your shoulder if you hear a sound
No mugging here, you are safe and sound
Back to Basics, marriage is for life
Even through the struggles and strife
The children have a Mum and a Dad
Life altogether isn't too bad
Back to Basics, is being able to work
With money in our pocket, we don't need to shirk
The children are taught to give up their seat
If someone older is standing and looks dead beat
The things you buy you look at with pride
No one will steal and go and hide
Back to Basics, is going back in time
Not as far back as the song *Buddy Can You Spare A Dime*
I don't think we can go *Back to Basics* again
It means all the progress has been in vain
There is too much cruelty and greed
We all want more than what we need
Forget the *Back to Basics,* it's just a dream
Unless we can find a very good team
I have no work, I'll have another hour in bed
Or I might go out and have a drink instead.
Cheers.

Marjorie Davies

BACK TO BASICS

Does Back to Basics now imply
No more lies or *pie in the sky*
No more silly speculations
And doubts about harsh regulations?
Teachers must uphold the law
Even those they do deplore
Is that not what they are paid for?
Neither must they act as mothers
Be counsellors: leave that to others.
Their chief role is to impart
Stability and love of art.

Will Back to Basics really mean
Just what it says, no in between?
All work will be well scrutinised
That without effort there's no gain
Even though it does mean pain
Even the ones that aren't too bright
Won't despair they'll see the light.
Common sense will prevail;
They won't on purpose choose to fail.
Then in the end, school might become
A place again where work was done.

Jill Ives

JUST WORDS

Reason together platform hounding
Division containing scarlet fire
Confound medical colour complaining
Neither compound further dire.

Statue statute inner meaning
Without outer boundary fly
Connect decision forever ever
Between cobalt crystal sky.

Singing dragon adept vortex
Eternity myth mystery gone
Enter return visit empire
Voyage journey staging one.

Heaven valley shining foreword
Night infinite island home
Open itself draw foundation
Stranger sunset weekend loam.

Sarah Ollerenshaw

ME ALONE

I remember the woman who was me, before you,
I wonder what happened, why she never grew,
But instead merged into married bliss,
Until brave enough to say 'I don't want this.'

Once single again, it took me time to find,
The personality that once was mine,
To face the World proudly and say 'This is me,
And I'm just who I wanted to be.'

I can see it in others, their faces they hide,
Try to pretend they're not who they are on the inside,
But instead create what they think their partner wants,
And what for . . . just a few isolated grunts.

I'm sure we'd all be happier if we could find,
Someone in our lives who appreciates our mind,
And lets us retain more of the *me* we once knew,
Not to leave *one* behind when we become *two.*

Lynn Michelle Hiller

BACK TO BASICS AND MCD

It's something I saw
in the paper
about that MCD
me and our Steven
for weeks now
have been deciding
whether to give up meat
for our tea
Linda McCartney Veg-Burgers
I will get
when I go into town
but my hubby,
I know for a start
upset will be his apple-cart
Veg-Burgers are not
his speciality,
it's easy to cook a beef joint
Monday stew
is more to his point,
OK me and our Steve
will give it a try
and hope that father will too
before mad cow
gets us all
and lands us all
in the stew,
so what shall we have for tea?
We might have to go
Back to Basics
we'll see.

Audrey Gamble

GOING BACK TO BASICS WOULD MEAN FOR ME

Going back to basics would mean for me
starting all over from scratch and the ABC.
A widow at my age going back to school?
It would make me feel seven kinds of a fool.

My punctuation marks are far from correct,
I could be a poet but for this defect.
Which I find it rather difficult to master
and bet I could learn Chinese backward faster!
Hopefully, I'll yet find an answer to it . . .
It's a do-or-die thing; I'll hang on to it.

Like mother, like daughter, like grand-daughter too,
at the back of my mind I felt, always knew,
our family hobby lives in my blood,
and I'd cultivate poetry - that I should.

Thus I am being pushed by my motivation
but feel bogged down by my punctuation.
I have a great philosophy; don't feel let down.
Who knows? Maybe one day yet I'll win a poet's crown.
Meanwhile if I get nowhere, no need to be sorry,
as it won't be yet the end of my story.

Having been to poetry a dedicated slave
I hope to have this inscription on my grave:
'Here lies Daniela K Ryan,
The greatest would-be poet in the universe.
Who wouldn't give up, but kept trying
and wrote this epitaph in her own verse.
Who of poetry has always been fond,
and hopes to go on writing in the Great Beyond.'

It's sort of going back to basics, one can say
and staring in another world, far away.

Daniela Ryan

NO TASTE

Begin to savour,
on the tip of the tongue,
sweet, sour, tangy,
cool, warm or hot.

Baby tentatively tries
button, striped wasp or pin.
Clenches lips 'gainst
foods or medicine spoon.

Childhood salt of tears,
clear fresh taste of rain.
Breathe catching mint,
nose tickling sherbet.

Young love, sweet kisses,
tongue on skin,
delicious sweat
intermingled heat.

All at last forgot,
Chocolate, chips, crisps,
rendered tasteless
in my smoke filled
toothless cavity.

Joan Fulford

BACK TO BASICS

Caught out by a major catch phrase
That sought to capture those halcyon days
When politicians were held in esteem
Strong, caring and squeaky clean

From this man in a dream with no vision
That attracts a stoic nation's derision
Cries from the unemployed, aged and sick
Answered with smiles and a glib statistic

Bills to bring tears to pensioners' eyes
Bills to Privatise, Fragment, and Franchise
The Mines, Railways, and National Health
Victims to feed a minorities' wealth.

Policies basically no longer sensible
Edicts immoral and incomprehensible
Common sense blurred by idealistic ideas
Get back to using your eyes and ears.

David Kennedy

BACK TO BASICS

There are smells of curry and garlic
And sizzling sounds in the air;
We're trying those new fancy dishes
Persuaded by two teenage girls.

But I must admit I can't bear it,
Those odours I find a bit much.
And so by the time it is ready
My stomach's beginning to lurch.

The girls are highly delighted
Eating curry and garlic with glee;
But those spicy foods give me the willies
So it's back to basics for me.

For dinner roast beef and potatoes
And a lovely green salad for tea,
With carrots, spring onions and peppers
Topped off with some fresh grated cheese.

Maureen Quirey

NEXT TIME

A spread of trees, dense undergrowth
covered all the land,
The ground beneath was dank and moist,
Just as mother nature planned.

Creatures roamed among the bush,
Evolved, from when time began,
They knew not that their downfall
would be from the animal, Man.

At first man made some clearings,
So in safety he could live,
And then he cut out pathways,
The ease of travelling for to give.

Man bred the fastest of them all,
And plundered everything in sight,
He cared not for the other beings,
He thought he had the right.

The land was cleared at such a pace
lots of creatures disappeared,
Gone was their home, their habitat,
As the humans' ugly head was reared.

In place of forest, sweet and fresh,
Town and cities did replace,
Instead of paths and narrow tracks,
Giant motorways grew apace.

Perhaps in many thousand years,
Maybe less, as to our shame,
As we destroyed one world for some,
To ours we'll do the same.

Then once again the barren wastes
will throng with creatures, safe and free,
And pray that the world's next masters,
Will make a better job than we.
David A Garrett

BACK TO BASICS

Back to Basics - what does this mean?
There's no universal definition, it would seem.
Is it to teach children to do what is right?
To love their neighbours and never fight -
And always, to everyone, be polite?

Is it to work hard at their sums
And always try to help their Mums?
Never to lie or cheat or steal
Trying to establish on earth - goodwill -
As always one's duty one tries to fulfil?

It is all of these qualities and more
That in all people the world's looking for.
But an incentive must be given
To turn earth's potential Hell to Heaven.

There's no good reason why anyone should
Try hard to live a life that is good
When selfishness seems to pay so well
Despite its effect on others is *Hell.*

Our nation must be taught again
That Almighty God be allowed to reign.
He has given us an Instruction Book
The Bible - in it we must look
As God, the Eternal *Basic* speaks
And says 'What man sows, so he reaps!'

This nation, it has turned from God,
Forsaking the pathway that Christ trod
And all our efforts will futile be
Unless as a nation we bow the knee
To God - The *First Eternal Basic.*

Jeanne Boffey

BACK TO THE FUTURE

And what is this Back to Basics
That they tell us is mighty fine?
Is it turn of the century values
That sent little boys down the mine?

Is it found in the twenties and thirties,
With recession and Bonnie and Clyde,
With the Reich and with Mussolini,
And if you were Jewish - you died?

And think of the nineteen forties
You get-back-to-basics dreamer,
I'll mention just two of the words,
Nagasaki and Hiroshima!

Is it found in the nineteen fifties
This return to the basic state?
Not in Alabama or Cape Town
Not even in Notting Hill Gate!

And what of the nineteen sixties
Did basic morality reign,
With Rachman, Profumo and Keeler,
And Beeching destroying my train?

Now I come to the seventies and eighties,
Starvation in Africa still,
Watergate, Heysel, Lord Lucan,
And in Ulster they kill and they kill.

The moral is, dear Prime Minister,
If you're looking for values that last,
Look forward with hope to the future
Don't hanker for myths of the past!

Peter Davies

BACK TO BASICS

Back to basics basically
Is the bottom of the tree.
Roots spread out to form a base
On which to build a human race.

Rising from these solid roots
Green and tender supple shoots
Pure, innocent and spry
Reaching upwards to the sky.

Influences then invade
Out from atmospheric shade.
Weather, seasons, dark and light,
Hours divided day and night.

Share resources as to need
Then invades pernicious greed.
Goodness strikes to quell this sin
Battles royal now begin.

Power shows its ugly head
Strength does govern, weaklings dead.
Cunning seeps from inner tree
To counteract humanity.

But sources good do then unite
To fight, fight, fight and fight,
But what is wrong? And what is right?
Virtue sidles into sight.

Stop the carnage, drop the gun,
Let the leaves imbibe the sun.
To procreate some decency
Back to basics it must be.

D Howlett

A PRAYER

Oh Lord who gifted us with life,
And for a dwelling gave this earth,
Our faith in Thee at times is shaken,
We see not then, a boon, our birth.
Would we might understand Thy deeds,
Why rich are some and others poor,
And fortune ill-distributed,
Continually knocks familiar door,
Why is it some achieve success
By minimum of effort made?
Whilst others toil unselfishly
Seeking the sun, yet finding shade.
As we believe that Thou art just,
Thy favoured ones perchance it be,
Required for higher service soon,
You strengthen by adversity.
And problems send them with each day,
To fortitude and courage test,
And prove at length their worthiness
To join the legion of the Blessed.
If this be so Lord, should the task
Be greater than our strength can bear,
And we should pray for help, please guide
Us from the brink of grim despair.
For though we know the path is straight
That ultimately leads to Thee,
The journey through this earth is hard,
For chained and shackled oft are we.
But may we hope each danger braved,
Each sorrow undergone,
Will snap one link from the fetter's chain,
And find us further on.

Vera Fertash

SCALE OF HOPE

There must be a balance
an equable level
to keep this good Earth a good place to live.
Man's intrinsic birthright,
this paramount asset,
deserves the impeccable care man can give.

Black oil is our bonus
don't waste it - Conserve it!
Don't let noxious poisons so recklessly kill.
Keep rain fresh - Not acid
Keep soil pure - Not tainted
Replace the reserves which we ransack at will.

Remember all creatures -
blue whale and sleek seal,
the lion and the leopard and elephant tall,
wren, eagle and lapwing
have their right to share in
this wonderful place - There is room for us all!

So nurture the wild flowers,
bees, butterflies, blossom -
Ensure that the fish spawn in sweet purity.
Safeguard crops grow cleanly,
that rivers flow clearly,
Green forests and pastures - The fathomless Sea

Must all be protected
kept free from pollution -
Restocked - Not neglected

For a Safe Destiny.

Rosemary Hankins

BACK TO BASICS (1950)

Happy childhood, innocent fun,
No mugging or rape, by knife or gun,
Mum at home, Dad at work,
Parental duties they did not shirk,
Guidance and values, taught, accepted,
Elders and authority to be respected,
School assembly paved the way,
To Christian attitudes of the day,
We did do wrong, we did commit sin,
But it was a safer society that we lived in
The biggest crime I can tell,
Scrump an apple, then run like hell!
If caught committing this dreadful crime,
A clip round the ear brought one back in line,
Do wrong at school, expect the cane,
Only the foolhardy misbehaved again,

Now life isn't governed by the rule,
Either in the home, or in the school,
No morality, no consideration,
No integrity, no expectation,
The vulnerable, exposed, abused,
Justice, no, you'll be excused,
Violence is getting worse,
Advanced technology has proved a curse,
Graphic details for all to see,
On computer, video and TV,
Let's get our priorities right,
Protect the children from this sight,
Then perhaps *normality* will reign,
And back to basics we can go again.

Heather Perrott

BASIC LIVING

Bare feet running
Beings crouched to their knees
Skins hanging sunning
Bodies flying through the trees.
Down in the glen an open fire
Surrounded by lots of hanging things
Roots and fish, meat and furs
All a good healthy life to bring
No canvas tents we see
But huts of twig and branches
While all around the children play
And adults sit on their haunches
Clad only in furs and skins
No animal rights people here
Only men crawling in line
That herd of deer to get near
To feed and clothe them all.
A primitive people it would seem
No! Only the twentieth century back to basics team.

Pat Duncan

BACK TO BASICS

'Excuse me, mate, we've lost our way
I think we've come too far.
It's *Basics* is the place we want
We should have come by car.'

'It's *back* to Basics you must go
The road is quite uphill
But with principles, you'll reach the top
And goals and aims fulfil.

The moral attitude you need
Was lost along the way
And must be found to make us all
Great again today.

So turn around and do your best
You've got to carry on
I'll be right here and be your guide
By the way, my name is John.'

V Tank

BACK TO BASICS

Back to Basics brings to mind,
Those precious things left behind,
Where has gone the helping hand
To old folks who can hardly stand,
In queues, or even climb on bus.
Back to Basics we really must.

Life is hectic rush and tear,
Time to chat is very rare,
Sometimes children take second place
As we all to work do race,
More money must we earn
To buy the things they do yearn.

Back to Basics we must go,
Meaning many things we know,
Gentleness and thought for others,
Taught to us by our dear mothers,
Kindness, and Friendliness to everyone,
Back to Basics soon must come.

Grace Woods

BACK TO BASICS

How many more around the world
Will suffer just like Biko.
Those men and women of peace,
Persecuted for their beliefs,
Who fight against corruption,
So all can share
With equal rights
The dignity of life, of love,
Of needs fulfilled.
The right to be treated as a human being.

The Berlin Wall was torn down
Families were united once more.
Russia has broken down the barriers.
The path to free speech is open.
Apartheid has been abolished
After many years of struggle.
Let us remember the lives lost.
Lives lost for freedom.
Let us celebrate those lives,
But not forget those still fighting.

Can we all help to end this inhumanity?
Can we start loving instead of hating?
Can we start sharing instead of grabbing?
Can we start caring instead of ignoring?
Those voices cry out from our own street.
Can we return to basic beliefs
That each man, woman and child
Has the right to basic needs fulfilled?
Let us in love honour each human life.
Let us in love change the world.

Josephine Blyth

W(H)ITHER THE LANGUAGE?

so you say we dont need capitals
for names not any more
forget fullstops and commas
punctuation is a bore
whoevers heard of gerunds
or what it means to parse
phonetic spelling is the mode
and what of split infinitives
such niceties are dead
to boldly go the nation knows
is how it should be said
dont worry over clauses
conjunction and pronoun
no one seems to realise
that due to needs a noun
out with formal language
self expression is what counts
be free and let the writing flow
in small or large amounts

However fine the thinking
Behind these current trends,
If they persist much longer
Communication ends
In reams of words quite meaningless;
Yet it's not too late to try.
Bring back spelling, grammar too,
Don't let our Language die!

Margaret Sargent

BACK TO BASICS?

Back to basics we are told
What exactly does this mean?
Treating folks like human beings
Keeping town and country green?

Caring for the older people
Making sure they're fed and warm
Helping those who are most needy
Out of trouble, free from harm.

Politicians all world over
Make rash promises to all
Then when fortunes start to dwindle
Truth is learned and heads may fall.

In this harsh and troubled world
Whom can we believe these days?
Nothing counts but making money
Life is grim in many ways.

Surely there must be an answer
Lessons now should be well learned
Faith and hope are what is needed
Charity should not be spurned.

People need to see a glimmer
Silver lining shining through
Looking toward a brighter future
Making way for hope anew.

Val Guttridge

THE BASICS OF LIFE

Gone are the days of yesteryear
when essential were the three R's,
reading, writing and arithmetic -
a firm foundation from the stars.

Three other important lessons
of which daily we had to learn
were discipline, respect and patience,
turn the other cheek and not to spurn.

Put pride into your actions do,
dress smartly with hair in place,
remember to try your very best
in everything - we're not in a race.

To show commitment throughout life
and marriage for ever the vow.
Through both the good times and the bad
talk, support each other, don't row.

Give freely your time to others,
offer a shoulder and helping hand,
walk before you run with your brothers,
listen to advice and understand.

Never spend if you can't afford to
you know money is not everything -
go outside, look around, enjoy the view,
see the wonders living can bring.

We all started life with no money,
to grow in love, harmony and trust.
Find the peace of the Lord - be happy,
yes the *basics* of life is a must.

Margaret Jackson

REFLECTIONS

I thought meself, the other day, -
'I'm *totting up* the years!
I'm at a time I can look back
O'er laughter, joy and tears.'
Ay, time was I listened to others' tales
Of Life - way in the past;
Seeing pictures through *their* eyes
So fleeting - hard to grasp!

Time has passed and, now I find
'Tis *me* who's telling the tales;
All of the time when *I* was young,
And life in my young days!
Wisely nodding, *marking my words* -
Giving advice re the bees and the birds;
All my opinions on experience based -
Just like me Mother, whose example I faced!

I note, with surprise, the many things past;
Result of progress - they just couldn't last;
Horse-driven ploughs, hay wagons and churns;
Milking by hand - cheese-making by turns -
These are the basics of which my life's made,
Now - to the Young - curios displayed:
For, - what seems to me, nought but a short while, -
A big slice of History we did compile!

Bee Wickens

BACK TO BASICS

To make a cake there has to be
A really basic recipe.
Ingredients must all be weighed
And balance with each other made.

They must be used in method stated,
And stirred and gently infiltrated.
If from these rules we choose to stray,
Such precious food is thrown away.

These basic rules should also be
Remembered well by you and me.
When in our lives from day to day
We strive to live in ordered way.

We know we cannot perfect be,
We're sometimes grilled by life you see.
But, as an oven must be watched,
Our misdemeanours should be scotched.

So, as the cake is proudly shown
Because we have the basics known,
Just let us try to live the same,
With *Back to Basics* as our aim.

Margaret Violet Hodgson

REMEMBRANCE DAY

The soldier lies in Flanders field
Muddied, bloody and dead.
There he sleeps Eternally
At rest in his earthly bed.

Before the Cenotaph another stands
With bowed dishevelled head
A wreath of poppies in his hands
His tribute to the gallant dead.

It worries not the warrior
He is not well dressed or smart
It is enough that he remembers him
With a true and thankful heart

To those who criticised the man
I have only this to say
'Twas his National Pride
Made him stand outside
And commemorate this day.

Maureen Mason

HOME FROM HOME

If you were to visit mum
Down Dorset you would come
Walk along the path that meets
An old cottage very sweet.

Just two little rooms you'll find
An open fire, the blackleaded kind
In the kitchen, bright and clean
Just the basics to be seen.

There is no freezer for this or that
No washing machine, just the cat!
Outside the back a lovely view
Beautiful garden but oh! The loo!

Mum loves it here and wouldn't roam
She will not budge with me to come
Times have changed I would agree
But home is home *basically*.

Beryl Smyter

THEN AND NOW

When I was young we used to have a tin bath outside the door,
And on Friday nights it was brought inside, and placed upon the floor
In front of the fire, then it was filled with water nice and hot,
And one by one we had our baths, topping up with hot water from
the pot.
We didn't have a loo inside, it was at the bottom of the garden,
And it was blinking cold in wintertime, but to this we grew quite
hardened.
We didn't have a telly, just a little radio,
And we'd huddle round the fireplace when cold winds began to blow.
We didn't have carpets on our floors, just lino and a mat,
And we had no running hot water, but we didn't mind about that.
If we made ourselves too dirty we got our backsides tanned,
'Cos we didn't have very many clothes, and all washing was done
by hand.
We always walked or rode our bikes, a car ride was a treat,
And who needed cars to get around when you had your own
two feet?
I'll turn up my central heating to keep me snug and warm.
I've got a new fitted kitchen, with microwave and washing machine,
And I can have a shower twice a day to keep me nice and clean.
I've got a TV set in every room, and carpets wall-to-wall,
I've a hi-fi and CD player, and a telephone in the hall.
There's fitted wardrobes in the bedrooms, and more clothes
than I can wear,
I've a Vax to keep my carpets clean, and a dryer for my hair.
So as I think of then and now, I'd like to make one thing clear,
You can all go back to basics, but me, I'm staying here!

June Stokes

BACK TO BASICS

Going back to basics
Is having parents rule
With Mother in the kitchen
When the kids come home from school.

She has time to stop to listen
While they tell about their day
No sitting in front of the telly
But time to read and play

Going back to basics
Is teaching right from wrong
As soon as *no* is understood
When children are still young

No point in blaming teachers
For bad manners in a child
It's the parents' responsibility
Though this may make some wild

Going back to basics
Is showing more respect
For other people's property
Not 'It's not mine so what the heck!'

Going back to basics
May come true one day
If we don't do what our leaders do
Only what they say!

J F Hunter

BACK TO BASICS

Modern technology leaves me cold -
Maybe I'm just getting old!
Not for me, cars that won't start -
I'd prefer a horse and cart!

Calculators I just dread -
I prefer to use my head
To add, subtract and multiply,
And I can't understand just why
We need to travel in the sky
When going places - life's too fast!
We've lost the pleasures of the past.
No time to stand and gaze a while,
No time to share a friendly smile.
It's rush and bustle all the time,
A simpler life would be sublime.

Let's go back to the old ways
And standards of the bygone days,
When people meant much more than things,
And find the happiness it brings

G Whittle

RURAL BASICS

Hey nonny no! Back to basics I go
After lunching with friends in the town.
We had a good time, a few glasses of wine,
And now my defences are down.

Hey diddle diddle! The cat's done a piddle
Just inside the front door.
The dog has done worse. My comments are terse.
I've trodden it into the floor.

Hey nonny no! Outside I go
To feed all the hens and the sheep.
The hens are okay, but O lack a day!
The ram's in the greenhouse asleep.

Hey diddle diddle! Like pig in the middle
I hardly know which way to go.
If I frighten the tup he's bound to jump up
And crash through the glass with one blow.

Hey nonny nay! I've enticed him with hay.
He's back in the field with the ewes.
I'll clean up the mess, and then, yes you've guessed,
I'll relax with a large glass of booze.

Ann Mather

BACK TO BASICS

In our lives we have ambitions
        this is so of Politicians,
They must look good to you and me
        when climbing their political tree.
'Let's get to basics,' said with vigour,
        'Basic what!' the other side snigger.
Let's get to basics seems the fashion
        tho' this is said without compassion.
Back to basics means to me,
        caring, trusting, loyalty.
Loyal to the ones who need,
        not the ones of power and greed.
Caring for the next generation,
        regardless of their colour or station.
Trusting in ourselves and others,
        giving love where no one bothers.
If we can share these basic things
        then we will see the change they bring.

M Burke

BACK TO BASICS

'We are moving' said my partner ' to the cottage of our dreams
        It nestles 'neath the snowy peaks of Wales
We'll generate our own electric, use the fire to cook our food
        And fetch water from the stream in wooden pails

Let's dispense with Supermarkets, eat only what we grow ourselves
        Then sell what's left in town on market day
No more lawns to cut each Sunday, the grass can grow waist high
        And we'll harvest so the animals have hay

Oh yes there must be livestock, pigs, goats, a flock of sheep
        Some chickens for their eggs, a cow or two
In the evenings you'll sit spinning and knit our winter clothes
        While I read old Farmers Weeklies through and through

We won't need a television, rule out the telephone
        Entertain ourselves with poetry and song
I can nearly play the guitar and voice is rather good
        We can make the words up as we go along

Oh Darling can't you see it, after toiling in the fields
        Trudging home to bathe before the open fire
It's really Back to Basics, it's what it's all about
        This plan has always been my heart's desire.'

But now I must confess to him this lothario of mine
        His rustic idyll holds no appeal at all
For while he sees me milking cows, chopping wood and baking bread
        I dream of melting plastic in the Shopping Mall.

June Ansell

MAYHEM

Are you bossed around by your kids?
Do you think they have flipped their lids?
What is wrong with the kids of today?
They are cheeky and rude and will not obey
Teenagers are a pain in the neck
Intent on making the home a wreck
All they do is cause trouble and strife
Taking over and ruling your life
Most of their day is spent in bed
Reluctantly getting up to be fed
Whatever they use - never put it away
Where it was used, there it will stay
It doesn't matter what you say
They argue wrong's right and get their own way
All they want is to stay up all night
Playing their music and ruining their sight
Watching *Telly* till early morn
Going to bed at early dawn
This World will really go to pot
When it is taken over by this lot.
More discipline is what they need
Till they change their ways and take heed
Of a little common-sense to recompense
Hurricanes, earthquakes, acts of God
He will step in on this World so *Mod*
The end of the World will surely come
Before God's work is finally done.
Give me strength O Lord I pray
That I may face another day.

Evelyn A Evans

GOODWILL SLEEPING

Sleeping hamlet, sleeping hamlet are you really true
Don't you see the progress of the town coming out to devour you?
No longer behind your armour of trees can you dare to hide
Though in peace today you slumber away out in the countryside.

Sleeping hamlet, sleeping hamlet oh! Why can't you see
With modernisation for everyone they will never let you be.
Already someone you don't know in a city far away
On paper has turned your narrow streets into a complex with cafe.

Sleeping hamlet, sleeping hamlet reconciled to die
With all your beauty and charm why don't they pass you by?
Instead of this with machinery they are going to lay you down
Then turn you into a nameless suburb of the growing town.

Sleeping hamlet, sleeping hamlet don't you see in your scope
That my friends and I together bring for you new life and hope?
With tenderness we will clean you up, your houses we will restore
Then without fear of the modern man you can sleep as before.

Sleeping hamlet, sleeping hamlet with the goodwill of modern man
After the fall of the tallest flats our children will still see you stand
Cloaked in ever growing foliage nature's creatures around you play
So sleep little hamlet for evermore so all may see you this way.

Christine Johnson

THE HOUR GLASS

Move back to basics, learn to scan,
with nature to care and plan.
Our lives thro' the hour glass fall.
Once we were, and did stand tall.

As dust now, mere grains of sand
returned are we unto the land.
Dust to dust, earth to earth.
Created for this and given birth?

Is all our toil, work and strife
an inconsequential part of life?
Or does each grain have its place
each on which another forms its base?

And so within this measured amount
every grain of sand doth count.
Adds to the passing of time
falling down that triangular line.

Whether famous or just mundane
all follow that similar plane,
and so to rest no matter what,
what they did or what they got.

Each has a vital part of play,
to measure the hours of the day.
What mark left you on yesterday?
To show you once passed this way?

Time is all; and all is time,
Standing still gives form to line!
For knowing is known; going is gone:
Some golden grains of sand shone.

So just what do you leave behind
for future generations of mankind?

H D Hensman

DIFFERENT TIMES

Looking back to yesterday
Can give us chance to see
The way we keep on changing
From the way we used to be

When doors could be left open
Go out without the fear
Of something being taken
From the home we love so dear

When kids could play in safety
Tipcat, whip and top
Without the fear of traffic
For the horses used to stop

When smoke went up the chimney
Living fire's burnt in the grate
And coalmen used to come around
To shout, 'A bag for one and eight'

When outside was the wash-house
The sound of Blub, blub, blub
As the women did their washing
With a dolly and a tub

When without machinery
Some things were done by hand
Yet those old crafts of yesterday
Can still stand out so grand

And one of the little things
That made our life worthwhile
Was the shop just on the corner
And the grocer with a smile.

Olive Walters

SHANK'S PONY

My ancient car is a joy to drive,
Well MoT'd, fully certified,
Visibly dented but the steering is tight;
It's an Austin Healey Sprite.
I took it on a trip to see my girlfriend late one night,
Some drunkard wrote it off and redesigned it,
Now I rely on Shank's Pony, the ability to hike,
Call it back to basics, if you like.

I borrowed a close friend's motorbike
To save my legs, salvage time,
I soon left the lorries and cars behind
With superior speed I'd lean to one side,
Once I took a tricky corner far too wide,
The machine and I parted company as it continued to slide
I have to crawl around my angry friend, walk instead of ride,
Call is back to basics, if you like.

Walking is time consuming, my legs get too tired,
It's okay in moderation, not all the blessed while,
Public transport is an answer though expensive in due time
With my financial disposition I need a cheaper ride,
That's how I reached the bold decision to acquire a pedal bike,
I got one on HP with a rear and front headlight,
I tried to scratch an itch on my back, I lost the bike in a dike;
It's definitely back to basics alright.

This poem's called *Shank's Pony*
Which may seem a little trite,
Call it *Back to Basics*
If you like.

Glenn R Lumb

BACK TO THE BASICS

Electric kettles
Electric knives
Microwaves
Electric lights
Washing machines spinning around
Keeping in time to the radio sounds

Must get some shopping
Let's take the car
It's just down the road, but that's really too far
To struggle along with the bags in your hands
It's a hard life we lead, you understand

Many miles away from our hectic life
There stands a village
Full of trouble and strife
Burning away under African sun
The mother struggles to get her tasks done
She beats the ingredients to make the bread
And walks to the well, with a pot on her head
Stretching the food to make it go far
Nobody here possesses a car

We think we're hard done by
That life is so cheap
But if we lived there, for only a week
We just couldn't cope
We'd be in a fix
In fact you could say
We'd be *back to the basics.*

Debbie Southon

THE GRASS IS ALWAYS GREENER!

To Pam, a pen friend

I envy you, living near Kew
In a flat towering high
With river close by
What a lovely view
From your window too
How I envy you, living near Kew.

And yet I see, you envy me
In country bound, with fields around
Where children play, quite safe, all day.
Our garden, with pleasure
Means work in good measure
While you at Kew, may admire the view
Without the need - to pick out weed!

How lucky we are, whether near or far
To love the earth, and see its worth
The joy it brings, to peasants and kings,
So let's agree, you envy me
And I envy you
Living near Kew!

Kate Fell

BACK TO FRONT

What *Back to Basics* means to me
Is a rethink of our ways
When times are hard and bleak we
Reminisce on the good old days

Back when people left their home
Unlocked at any hour
Back when kids could safely roam
And leave whole tree and flower

Now conversation's long since dead
Preceded by the telly
With half the population fed
And half with empty belly

Our politicians serve us not
Don't follow by example
With unemployment as our lot
And pensions less than ample

The health service is crippled too
With beds put up for sale
The rich are first in every queue
Thus goes this sorry tale.

The answer lies not in the past
But in the people living
Back to Basics should be recast
To mean less take more giving.

Claire Robinson

BACK TO BASICS

There are *wrongs* and *rights* in everyday life
When young, we were shown how to hold a fork and knife
Not to tell lies, be tidy and to the old, be kind
And if we were naughty, got a good smacked behind!
We didn't expect or demand presents beyond Dad's means,
And we didn't wear those awful scruffy torn jeans.
We were happy playing out - kicking tins, skipping,
enjoying hide and seek,
Our friends at school were great - no bullying - the strong
cared for the weak.
How times have changed over the last sixty years -
Maybe we *wrinklies*, who are on our way out, won't see the
fear on parents' faces
If they taught their children good manners - they'd get *back to basics.*

Sheila Stead

BASIC PARENTING

Listen parents, listen!
Hark to the voice of youth,
Crying to you for guidance,
Begging to know the truth.

They come to you as innocents
Straight from the lap of love,
Don't let them be taught by others
Who do not know what is good.

Temper thy rod with kindness,
Let actions speak not words.
Love in unity bindeth,
A fold that will not unfurl.

Praise them when they need praising,
Teach by example please.
Lead them by firmly blazing,
A path that the blind could see.

Build them a home with courage
And love and honesty there
Cushion them with tenderness
Strengthen them with prayer.

Pat Barrett

BACK TO BASICS

We need to get back to basics
Found in the Word
When the name of God
Was highly revered

People then knew right from wrong
And lived life by a moral code
Always listening for the voice of reason
And showed respect and care for the old

Spare the rod and spoil the child
Has turned out to be true
Some can't think of anything bad enough
They don't know what to do

Kids like the thrill of a joyride
Glue sniffing or a trip on speed
These they find exciting
They help fulfil a need

There's something missing in our world today
So much disease sickness moral decay
It's too high a price to pay
It's time we put God back into our society.

Lorraine Hemphill

BACK TO BASICS

Let's get back to basics
The politician said
But what exactly does this mean
Should single parents wed

We could go back to the old days
When pregnant girls were forced
To marry their lives were miserable
Because it was a sin to get divorced

Should women stay at home all day
Chained to the kitchen sink
While their husbands work ten hours
Then go to the pub for a drink

Back to basics what do they mean
Is it the days of bread and ham
A steaming bowl of broth
And for afters toast and jam

Morality is declining
Crime is on the increase
Countries are fighting civil wars
Will there ever be any peace

Should we bring back hanging
Canning or the birch
Corporal punishment in schools
Be forced to go to church

Politicians should set a good example
That is what is expected
They should get their lives in order
If they want to be respected.

Margaret Haste

BACK TO BASICS

Exotic land for just one week
Strange culture quite bizarre
Oriental stunning location
Time passed like a falling star

Argued with an arrogant king
Chatted to a royal queen
A crown prince kissed my hand
How unrealistic was the scene

My accolade for all to see
A velvet night made for romance
With powerful and commanding voice
The king asked 'Shall we dance?'

Two hundred people perhaps more
Cheered as alone I stood
One brief moment's happiness
A triumph for our drama group

It's back to basics, very sad
Crash to earth like an alien comet
Face up to life's realities
Try and smile for the moment

Remember to pay the 'phone bill
Tidy the kitchen, mop the floors
Post letters, 'phone the office
Endless list of mundane chores

Must have a cup of coffee
'Phone rings a tired 'Hello'
'Oklahoma sounds exciting'
Another opening, another show!

Flora M Cameron

THE SCISSORS

Placing my fingers through
Two holes, I hold
My mother's scissors,
Remembering
I had been denied their use,
They had always been taboo
To a small child
Who, coveted them.
Remembering how I'd climbed a chair
Where, they were hidden,
The forbidden.
In a drawer, before
Clutched tightly to my chest
I'd jumped dangerously down
To reach the floor,
Then hide beneath the table.

I was able to peep through the
Bright red chenille of the cloth
That covered the hiding place.
All around the edge they hung
Red pom-poms that gaily swung
So temptingly to one so young.
I cut them off. Every one!
Turned to my brother
Who had joined me there,
Cut off his hair
By the time that I was found
In little mounds
Just everywhere a tangled mess
The mixture lay, reds and browns.

I remember getting smacked,
Oh, how I cried.
Not for the cutting damage done,
But what I'd said - I lied
With scissors still clasped in my hand,
I said 'It wasn't me,' quite earnestly
At the very tender age
Of three. I learnt a right from wrong.

Doreen Shand

TAILORING TALK

Would you like to be a tailoress
My mother questioned me
If you can sew you never will starve
Was mum's philosophy
And so I joined the many girls
Who chose to do this work
The hours were long, eight till six
But we never thought to shirk.
Accomplished sewers were found in Leeds
On that you could depend
Famous factories with famous names
Garments worldwide they would send
Over fifty years I now look back
And remember the words mum spoke
Over fifty years of sewing clothes
From dressmaking to bespoke
I look at the prices in the shops
Of clothes I would like to own
With nice material and a pattern
A new dress and jacket soon will be sewn
It's back to basics remembering still
The skills I learned whilst young
When at fourteen I readily joined
The busy tailoring throng.

Mary L Burton

BASIC LIFESTYLE

We're moving house today
and throwing out some things
We are going back to basics
To see what the change will bring

Out will go, the video and the satellite dish
The TV and the stereo
In comes books, and route maps
to fulfil our dearest wish

To be without these luxuries
will be a trial indeed
The microwave, the washing machine.
We won't really need

The car must go I'm sorry to say
Despite protestations from my wife
But how on earth can we keep it
if we're starting a brand new life

But what can we do the children cry
We've no computer games to play
I'm sure you'll find something to take its place
There was nothing like that in our day

We'll find little jobs that need to be done
and then we can sit and talk
Then if there's still some daylight left
We will all go for a walk

Our life's too precious to lounge about
and waste away our time
Come sit with me, just for a while
and I'll read you my new rhyme.

Colin Mills

BACK TO BASICS

This means at the beginning,
Before embroidery or trimming,
Not embellished - really plain -
Could even be - well - *Plain Jane.*

It is a very basic cake,
One that any child could make;
Just a very simple recipe -
But enjoyed by you and me.

Plain wallpaper and paint;
Unmarked without a taint.
Furnishings without some trimming,
Mother's figure without slimming!

Silence in the early dawn.
Gardens simply with a lawn,
No flowers blooming round the edge,
No plantpots on the window ledge.

Window panes without a drape,
No fancy curtains made of crepe;
No lounges with a *telly* playing,
No video for tapes replaying.

Baths without enamel on;
Floors with just linoleum.
There is no shower or shampoo -
A quick rub down for me and you.

No lovely shiny motor car
Standing there for *ma* and *pa* -
A bicycle just made for two -
That's transport for me and you.
Back to Basics's many things -
Time can alter everything!

Margaret Hooper

CIRCLES WITHIN CIRCLES

Basic needs are the necessities of all animal life,
It is not only human beings, who are subject to needless want
and strife,
All flora and fauna are basic to Earth's environmental needs,
Stretching from the rain forests of the Amazon, to the
garden's common weeds.

When man interferes with Nature, he inflicts immeasurable harm,
He deprives us by his greed, and robs Earth's natural charm.
Does he stop to think or consider, or even ask the reason why,
As his fossil fuels keep smoking, destroying ozone in the sky.

There is cruel hunting of fox and hare, some even call it a sport,
What kind of people are they, that show so little thought,
They show no respect for our wildlife, or indeed their basic need,
All they see is their own ego's, coupled with a selfish greed.

And what of those nations, who hunt innocent dolphins and whale,
Destroying the marine life of our oceans, as their horror ships
set sail,
Will they never ever realise, or ever see that distant light,
For these mammals of our oceans, they kill their basic right.

Scientists in laboratories, seeking out those hidden secrets of nature,
Experimenting testing and searching, conducting trials until
they're sure,
Discovering new answers, and producing vaccines by the score,
Those basic needs of all humanity, is what they are working for.

What about the senseless slaughter, in lands not so far away,
Surely it is a basic right of all people, to live and have their say,
Killing of the innocent, is mindless, savage and cruel,
Why can't they heed their intelligence, and respect those
basic rights of all.

As our Earth revolves and orbits, around our star we call the sun,
For man his arrival on the planet, it seems has only just begun,
No one knows how long we will rule, but now our time has
come to lead,
Time to recognise our planet's worth, and not destroy its basic need.

Jim Wilson

BACK TO BASICS

If we could only get back to basics,
As we did after World War Two,
We'd have a lot of work to do
And enjoy low prices too.

When we have reached zero inflation
And allowed it to settle for a time,
Then aim at percentage deflation
And let wages and profits decline.

With lower priced exports expanding,
Our world trading income would rise
Unemployment would soon be a thing of the past
And we would all take a share of the prize

Electrical power now costs thirty times more
Than it did at the end of the war;
We pay ninety times more for a ton of coal
And cigarettes fifty times more.

Now we are all buying more than we can really afford
And we are having to borrow the money
That's why we're fifty billion in debt every year
And we all know that's not very funny

But let's not Lamont, let's get back to basics
Though we haven't Hurd just Howe to do it
But a Major change has got to take place,
If it doesn't we will all live to rue it.

Morton Rock

BACK TO BASICS

Progress, technology, forward we strive
Busy and buzzing like bees in a hive
Onward and upward and never a thought
When the people less able to cope, become fraught.

Latest is best, if it's trendy or new, who cares anymore, when
those bills become due
It isn't a case of: I'll pay when I can, these days somebody
else always carries the can.

I want it I'll have it, today's attitude
Can't afford it? I'll steal it, too often the mood
Are your working? Why should I? Back comes the reply
Who's responsible now? No, not me. No, not I.

When I was a youngster, not all that long since, people cared
about people and they were convinced
That the family came first, second third fourth and last and the
dreams of the future were shaped by the past.

So we need to get back, basic standards of life
Basic discipline, order, not rule of the knife
When you work, keep the fruits of your labour and pain
If you don't, at least try, basic pride to sustain.

One thing we can all do, like ancestors before, is to sit down
each day, all together once more
For a meal and a chat, 'bout the day and its deeds, to talk eat
and listen, to all of our needs.

It's important for children to talk and to feel
How it's right to be good and it's quite wrong to steal
Or to borrow without the real owner's consent
And to live in a house and not want to pay rent.

If they learn basic morals, from parents and elders and see their
Dads working as fitters or welders
then find Mum at home, when they come back from school, with
a butty or drink, cold or hot when it's cool.

We can learn from the past, when we all had much less
Of material things, like fridge freezers and stress
But much more social conscience and pride in our lot
Don't know quite where we're going! Back to Basics, it's *not!*

Jane Hewitt

THE WRITINGS ON THE WALL

Strolling the canal.
I saw something quite banal.
Writing on the wall.
Graffiti of course, on the brickwork of the bridge.
Not porn, but a question asking what is the norm?
Another quip said _ _ _ _ four letter word (   ) this two a game of chess
The meaning could be anyone's guess,
Would to meet the author perchance to digress!
What wit, it is ever present.
Some more said, Poll Tax still not paying yet
And in large white letters, Kill Thatcher dead.
And Major Road ahead. Stop. Go. Stop.
Anarchy rules OK
Painted with a big eye
And yet again another gem
The peace sign symbol.
Underwritten
You will die not them.
Nevertheless, to that
Under my breath I muttered Amen.
Deep down, feeling bitter, thinking what a mess.
And is there any answer,
Besides the desecration of the bridge
And in the water litter.
Yet people had tried, and do.
I would not be enjoying this walk if not pleasant.
But oh, how your hands feel tied.

Thomas Charles Rimmer

WOULD I WANT TO GO BACK?

When I glance around my home - at all the things I own,
I realise that, just like others, I take it all for granted.
There are soft tissues and kitchen paper,
Cooking foil and clingfilm too.
There's a special solution for cleaning the bath -
And another for washing the floors.
A machine takes care of the dishes
While another deals with the linen.
The fridge and freezer are tightly packed
With all kinds of good things to eat.
My fruit bowl is overflowing, and there's plenty of wine in the rack.
And yet - it isn't so very long ago that my lifestyle was totally different.

In those better days - as some would say -
For me - well I'm not really too sure.
With my arthritic hands I would find it too hard
To scrub and ring out the washing,
And although I love tasting home baked bread
I never could knead it again.
But worst of all (for me that is)
Was bringing in the floor cloth - from where it hung on the linen line,
For to my horror each time - out would crawl at least half a dozen of the biggest earwigs of all!
But as for food - well that may be different, perhaps I would go back,
Even to salted dripping on bread - and cod liver oil on a spoon.
For then there were no additives, or chemicals in our food
Just fresh green vegetables with the meat,
And plenty of pie and custard,
With not the slightest hint - that we were getting too much cholesterol!

Jean Larner

BACK TO BASICS

Enid you brought us lots of love
From all those miles above
Arrived on Christmas Day
We were there to meet you
On our special day.

Standing there with coat and hat,
for you Enid to brave our cold,
The last book about Australia,
Had just been sold.

Homeward bound we travelled happy as can be
Waiting to open our presents round the Christmas tree

Together we are, since nineteen years
With mum and all four daughters
Our days are planned until the sixth
And on that day the snow did lay
Enid made a snowman.

Now the afternoon has ended
It is time to go
The drive to the airport
Will be very slow.

Snowflakes are still falling
The roads are very bad
Nearly to the airport
We all feel very sad.

Enid dear we don't want you to part
We have got to back home without you
But when your plane is above us right from the very start
We all love you
From the bottom
Of our hearts.

Ivy Kisbee

BACK TO BASICS

Back to basics, a political theme,
People are wondering, 'Now what does this mean,'
It means family values of love in the home,
It means loving parents, not wanting to roam.

To educate children in which class or creed,
To give all a chance, from poverty be freed,
New schools and new books, should be *their* first aim,
Put the Great back in Britain and save us from shame.

No sleeping in boxes on cold winter nights
No begging for food, near great cities lights,
No mentally ill patients, thrown out on the streets,
Bewildered and frightened of strangers they meet.

We ought to look after the old and the frail,
Who are not able to cope with life's bumpy trail.
Find time for a prayer, God will listen always
Let's stop all this heartache by mending out ways!

K Hart

BACK TO BASICS

Back to Basics - a welcome sound,
Get the three R's off the ground.
Concentrate on things worthwhile,
An end to all this time of trial.

The *integrated day* is really out,
No more time for playing about,
Reading readiness is now old hat,
No more waiting about for that.

Learning to read is a serious task,
Practise each day is all we ask,
To conquer sounds and word-building,
Are aids to help the skill of reading.

Writing must be neat and clear,
Well-formed letters now appear,
Correct spelling in full measure,
Gives the reader added pleasure.

Arithmetic is really fun
If the teaching is well done,
Tables taught right from the start,
Never forgotten if learnt by heart.

So back to basics every day,
When work is work and play is play,
Achievement the aim of everyone
To gain the praise for work well done.

Mary Stace

BASIC BEHAVIOUR

Basic behaviour patterns,
should be taught in schools.
A little discipline for kids,
intent on breaking rules.
An eye for an eye, a tooth for a tooth.
A good judicial measure.
Instead of detaining criminals
at Her Majesty's pleasure.
Why can't life nowadays
be like it was before?
When we could safely go to bed
without shutting the door.
When the government stopped the strap,
they were out of touch.
So now kids are allowed
to get away with far too much.
Back to basics we must go
if we're to win this war.
A little discipline for kids,
intent on breaking the law.
Tracey Anne Toma

IF ONLY

Do unto others as you would
That they should do to you.
Be honest in the things you say
And in the things you do.

The Greatest Man who ever lived
Has said it, as we know.
O Love your neighbour as yourself,
If only it were so.

If parents trained their children to
Respect those who are old
They would not burgle or knock down,
But help them in the cold.
If people did not peddle drugs
And sell them to a child
There would be less unhappiness,
Parents would not get wild.

If teenagers loved car owners
And their cars did not steal;
If sawn-off shotguns were not used,
Sore quarrels then could heal.

If papers would not publish what
They would not wish to see
Written about their families
A difference there would be.

The papers would be full of joy
Instead of full of woe,
The happiness of families
Would strike one with its glow.

We could return to basics then,
If only it were so.

Joyce M Turner

BACK TO BASICS

Drive around the car park, search for a space,
Scurry through the raindrops at a frantic pace,
Revolving door manoeuvre with trolley obstinate
Start on the trek of modern housewife's fate.

Cereals by the dozen, washing powders by the ton,
Discerning out to be on the vital shopping run,
Bottles in their hundreds to clean and sanitise,
Options so abundant in a scheme to tantalise.

Diverse all the contents, stacks and rows of tins,
Wrappers, cartons, boxes, a feed for rubbish bins,
Convenience food so tempting, there in profusion,
Shelves overflowing to breed much confusion.

Choices place in trolley, dodge around the aisles,
Queue at checkout, on counter put in piles,
Transfer all to bags with the ringing of the till,
Plunge back into trolley and settle up the bill.

Trundle off to car park with great larder loot,
Again transfer the carriers, hoist them in the boot,
Eventually get home, the final lap for stock
With kitchen shelves augmented, tensions can unlock.

Thoughts then of my mum as I sip a cup of tea,
Her grocer came to call, to keep her lugging free,
Tea? Sugar? Butter? Then marge, lard and cheese,
He cued for her order, her choice made at ease.

Handling goods just once to fill a pantry space,
When grocer had delivered, a transaction of such grace.
That *back to basics* order, oh, a dream of delight,
Extra hours of leisure not a trolley hassle fight.

Lydia Thomas

FAMILY LIFE

How times have changed in recent years
With mothers carving out careers
No-one there to calm their fears
Or mop away the frightened tears.
Children ever on the run
No mum at home to make life fun
No welcome there when school is done.
Children would not be a mess
If time spent home was more - not less!
There is no kiss and no caress
When they achieve exam success.
If there was more to family life
They wouldn't get in so much strife
And mugging wouldn't be so rife.
Children must be given time
Let's vindicate increasing crime
And know just where to draw the line.
Home is where a mum should be
For when they fall and graze a knee
It's *your* responsibility.
All their worries you should meet
So keeping children off the street
The violence then may well deplete.
What back to basics means to me
A stable, close-knit family
The children who become latch-key
Will get in trouble - naturally
I'm sure all children would be glad
If they could talk to mum *and* dad
This world would not be quite so bad.

M Mason

DOING THE WASHING

Blowing madly on the line
No effort from me required this time
Just pop it in the automatic washing machine
Watch it go round and sit and dream.
Sitting in the launderette
You don't even get your hands wet
Going back to days before
Monday was the day for this chore
Sunday nights you filled the copper
Laid the fire under the copper bottom
All the rubbish from that week
Went up in smoke to build up the heat
On the kitchen table the galvanised bath
Sunlight soap no detergent
Dolly board a job and a half
Boil it long starch it well
White as snow with the blue bag's powers
This job took just hours and hours
No time to get a proper dinner
Out came the frying pan
Sunday leftovers in it
No plug in iron or helpful aids
The kitchen range provided the heat
For the flat iron's used no time for treats
On the wooden clothes horse to air
After all that just sink exhausted in a chair
It was really hard work compared to todays
Thanks to modem technology we have changed our ways.

M Baxter

THE WHEEL MIGHT TURN FULL CIRCLE

On the seventh day God rested, and Earth's rent was
long contested,
But at last, Man signed the lease, with one great clause,
Come year two thousand's dawn, then the land must be re-born,
And returned to Eden's state, with yet no flaws.

Year dot and Man moved in, along with neighbours, greed and sin,
And fanned out upon the planet, like a vine,
There was plenty there for all, but too often came the call,
'That's not yours, I say, it's mine, it's mine, it's mine.'

Kindness died and Men fell craven, gone forever the safe haven,
And money ruled as Mother Nature's bane,
Ozone layer ripped asunder, oil deposits? . . . Let us plunder,
We even added acid to the rain.

My, haven't we evolved, and not one real problem solved,
Like . . . How can we clean up the poisoned seas?
Or maybe write a thesis, how we destroyed ten thousand species,
And still managed to wipe out a million trees.

Drop the waste in outer space, it offends the human race,
But the time is coming for the race to end,
And we must pause in thought, for that lease was dearly bought,
And the clause is broken, small real chance to mend.

Let's consider now the cost, what we had, like fools we lost,
But the wheel might turn full circle, ere we die,
Bid adieu, atomic feasts, welcome nature and all beasts,
'Give Man another chance . . . please God.' we'll cry.

To stop pollution winning, we must revert to our beginning,
Back to basics . . . stop the rot . . . it's not too late,
We're killing where we live, the Earth's nothing left to give,
Self destruct could be the verdict of our fate . . .

Jackaline Dorsett

CHANGING VALUES

Back to basics, a simple phrase, reminds one of the good old days,
When family life was a valued thing and father our guide on
many things
His rules were always strict yet fair, surveying the world from
his favourite chair.

Mother worked from morn till night, her nature happy warm
and bright
Ready to give a helping hand and very often in demand
Caring and cleaning every day, this was the accepted way.

Baking was a busy day, bread and cakes lined on a tray
Coming home to scones and jam and if lucky maybe ham
Pure white washing on the line, hoping the weather would be fine.

Today life is easier that is true, no bowls of starch or dolly blue
Yet values have vanished, what a shame, is the government
to blame?
More income tax and VAT both must be paid by such as we.

Petty crime and murder too, what can our police force do?
Drivers move at a high speed rate, at traffic lights they dislike
the wait
Car exhaust fumes fill the air, nobody has a moment to spare.

Jobs are scarce and far apart, young people just can't get a start
Miners signing on the dole, not needed now to hew the coal
Reports of war reach us each day, scenes of violence and affray.

Can life go on like this each day, hurting and killing in this way
Pray for life to improve, once more, prayer to open
progression's door
High standards to obtain, back to basics, once again.

Joan Parr Pearse

A REASON TO LIVE

Getting back to basics what reason can we give
What elementary substance for this life we live
A universe of humans struggling hard to find
A fundamental answer along with all mankind
We will persevere though battle torn and weary
To reach a conclusion, decide on fact or theory
What is the meaning of this life we live
Birth's a new beginning reproduction we give
The learning process the first faltering steps we take
The golden rules we learn most of which we break
From child to adult we take it all in our pace
Tell me why are we here the whole human race
What is our purpose to live in this world
Does anyone know will it all be unfurled
The mystery of existence how long will it last
Can somebody tell us, someone from the past
Is it really to earn a place in Heaven above
Then in the right direction please give me a shove
Is there an aim a force or a reckoning
To show us the way is the Lord there a-beckoning
Give me a reason and no more would I ask
I just need a cause to emerge from this mask
If nobody knows why we are here on this Earth
What's the point of this life no reason for rebirth
So for an answer I'm seeking to strive
Won't somebody please tell me why I'm alive.

Carol Anne Burnup

MY MOTHER

I had just a brief encounter
With her in childhood's hour
For she died at the age of forty two,
Yet she still lives and directs me in what I do.

She taught me to be humble and to pray to the lord.
She always reminded me there is only one God.
She said, 'The Bible is a book about life,
Read it my child and in Christ you'll believe.'

What a wonderful memory she's left me,
At my side she will always be,
I know she is with the Redeemer
Christ called her to serve him and the Father.

And as I sit each Sunday in chapel
Any doubts that I have she is dead I dispel,
I only have to open the hymn book and sing
Then I am reminded she is with the King.

I sincerely give thanks to her for my faith
For I am glad I listened and was taught the truth,
I will try and honour her memory
By showing kindness, gentility, generosity and humanity.

And when my earthly work is done,
May we meet in the Kingdom of the Holy One,
I know he will unite us much more together
Until that day comes the Bible's message I'll deliver.

Wilma Harris

'BACK TO BASICS'

'Back to Basics', is the cry,
  But what *does* this phrase imply?
Do our leaders really see,
  Where is real priority?
Should restrictions much increase,
  To enforce them, more police?
No, the Bobby on the Beat
  Is an answer incomplete.
We look to another law,
  Where there is solution sure.
Man must love our God, to start
  From within the Human Heart.
He should love his neighbours too,
  So God wishes him to do.
If he does this, he will live
  And God will his blessings give.
When God's love is in man known,
  Could he take what's not his own
And if God reigns perfectly,
  In the tongue can poison be?
Where would be desire or will
  To harm others, or to kill?
Evil never can be done
  In the presence of God's son.
He will for his neighbours care
  And his blessings seek to share.
With others he will congregate,
  On God's love to concentrate.
Then, all round, a light may shine
  Showing that great love divine.
'Back to Basics', there's the need,
  But the Lord himself will Lead.

Anon

JUNIOR SCHOOL IN THE 1930's

The whistle blew at five to nine
We children marched in line by line,
Hung up our coats on cloakroom hooks
Sat in our places, took out books.
A hymn was sung, a prayer was said,
A passage from the Bible read.

No time was wasted we begun
to learn our tables one by one.
Sums followed, adding, take-away,
Our concentration must not stray.
Next composition, what to write
upon a new page clean and white.

We only had one teacher. She
controlled us with authority.
I will not tell how with a cane
she caused considerable pain.
Suffice to say, before too long
we soon discovered right from wrong.

We used to run and dance and play
Out in the playground every day.
With skipping ropes and bags of beans
We formed up into several teams.
Oh! how I loved the daily 'drill'
With much delight I mind it still.

Our education! - very broad,
We never had time to be bored,
With reading, writing, spelling, singing,
Our childish voices upward winging.
We worked until the clock struck four
them tumbled out the old school door.

Margaret Aitken

BACK TO BASICS

The sun sinks low o'er the bone-hard field
Poor light signals the end of play
Bales are lifted and batsmen yield
Seven more runs would've won the day

Half a league to the finishing line
A second wind an' a quickened pace
Are all that's needed to beat the time
To put him into a medal place
The push and strain of the angry pack
Are all in vain in the clinging mud
For time has beaten their last attack
As it runs out with their sweat and blood

There's a eerie quiet as he starts his roll
Tension's felt all around the green
For the 'Jack's' protected by his rival's bowl
Which is also blocking his final dream

The cry of the cox rings in the ears
Of the men who strain to his counting pace
Their aching hearts and backs and fears
Are pushed to the limit to win the race

A 'birdie's' needed at the final hole
Nothing less can win the round
A fearsome drive and an awesome chip
Then a perfect putt will have to be found

The final frame and a blackball fight
The cushioned ball's now becoming a curse
Honour even at the end of the night
Now whoever pockets will take the purse

Norman Whittle

BACK TO BASICS

What do back to basics mean?
It seems that is only a dream
The world is so open-eyed
And we have to look hard for any pride.

Everyone is so of self,
We sit by ourselves like little elves,
Too greedy in this materialistic world,
Sometimes it's like we would loose our soul.

Liberty, Liberty
Sometimes I wish it was me
You see I am just little too shy,
But it seems they are the ones that get by.

It is just unclear to me,
What we are expected to be,
A virtuous kind and loving heart,
But these Officials do not play their part.

You see vandals are set free to roam,
They seek to vandalise old people's homes,
Tell me could this ever be right?
When the old and feeble are dying of injuries and fright?

I think something should be done,
People are supposed to live happy and have fun,
Caring for each other and enjoying life the best we can,
Though It's not at all easy on the wages and pension we have, in hand.

Our Officials we rely on for guide,
But they themselves have taken us for a ride,
Our hospitals and amenities are curtailed from us,
And then they call it some little cuts.

I would say back to basics in schools,
With children singing hymns and basic prayers as a rule,
To the assembly they should all march in,
Before any lessons begin.

Before they take their leave to go,
On buses, trains or whatever,
Again in the evenings too
It should be important as they grow.

Our children are shaped in our churches or schools,
And it should ever be the rule,
You know they will look back on these happy days,
As the beautiful fields, and the flowers on the trees.

Mrs M Joseph

BACK TO BASICS

I wish I had married an Indian Brave -
just think about all of the money I'd save.
No gas bills or taxes, no mortgage or rent -
wear buckskin and moccasins, live in a tent.

No shopping at Tescos for something to eat -
it's down to the old man to bring home the meat.
Just get the fire going then sit in the sun -
bung the meat in the pot and wait till it's done.

I'd bathe in the river then paint up me face -
whoop-it-up round the bonfire at Saturday raves.
Then back to the tent where a headache I'd pose -
(his dirty old feather gets right up my nose!)

His name? Something manly like 'Fight to the Death' -
but then again what if it's 'Buffalo Breath'.
The smell in our tent could become most unpleasant -
Er ... Forget all I've said - I'll stick with the present.

Janet Lomax

INSTRUCTIONS

If you buy a hi-fi; a tele; or a gram;
It comes with full instructions
So you don't get in a jam.

If you want to make a cake,
Some bread, or Christmas pud;
You follow the instructions,
So you can make it good.

Why then do we see no need,
Of instructions how to live,
But go through life so carelessly,
Not a glance at them we give.

Our maker gave instructions
The basic rules of life
But man thinks he knows better
That's why there's so much strife.

So take your Bible off the shelf,
And blow the dust away,
The basic rules are there for you,
So read them and obey.

Doreen Higgs

WHY HAS MAN BECOME SO GRAND

Imagine that there were no things,
No machines or piercing noise,
In days gone by people lived this way,
And thrived on simple joys.

Their music was the birdsong
Or a whistling farmhand's tune,
But in these busy, rushing times,
There simply isn't room

For peaceful thoughts
And gentle talks,
And tender silences.

Caught up in this mad, modern world we find
So little chance to soothe the mind
And dwell awhile in Nature's land
Oh why has man become so grand?

Jenny Eleftheriades

BACK TO BASICS

The term back to basic's has taken a lot of whipping.
Does it mean then we'll be back eating bread and dripping.
I don't think we can go Back to Basic's overnight.
To times when most people were honest and polite.
To me they just grab more money from yer purse.
And select certain ill folk to be attended by the nurse.
They have taken Back the Basic's by refusing to employ.
And now the sight is gone of a kid playing out with a real toy.
Most people don't seem to have now what cost's nothing to give.
To teach their kids that honesty pride and dignity is the only way to live.

Politicians create conditions where ordinary folk have no gain.
They have taken some folks dignity and washed it down the drain.
It's they who run the country and tell us what to do.
So what is Back to Basic's for them they haven't got a clue.
Why then don't they practice all of what they preach.
What is good for all of them we will never reach.
Back to Basic's comes from what you teach a young child.
And maybe then there would not be so many running wild.
It all boil's down to learning the right from the wrong.
Not the words of election hype off some politician's tongue.

Carol Lidster Wood

'BACK TO BASICS'

The PM talked a lot about 'getting back to basics'
  But no-one said just what those 'basics' mean.
Is it economics, food and housing or education?
  'Basics' can cover almost every scene.

Take economics. What we spend depends on what we earn,
  To the poor it means surviving every day,
Enough to keep a roof over the family's head
  And 'Basic food' to keep the wolf at bay.
'Basic food is definitely not the kind we see
  When they show us all those banquets on TV
It's meat and veg, sausages, or maybe fish and chips
  With plenty bread, and a nice hot cup of tea.

If they mean education, the 'basic' things will be
  Reading, writing and of course mathematics too,
Religious education, science and PE
  If you're good they'll make an athlete out of you.

But 'basics' also mean those fundamental things,
  Those that make all of our lives worth while.
Like good health, happiness, and best of all security,
  They're the 'basic' things to make us smile.
Although the old song tells us, 'The best things in life are free'
  The things that we like best cost lots of money,
We're tired of bills and taxes, and all long to be free,
  Forget Basics! Let's find a land that's *Sunny* !

Hannah M French

BACK TO BASICS

My life was so busy from morning 'till night.
I raced in my car, through the traffic, to work.
I shopped in my lunch hour, it felt like a fight
To get back for a drink - to give me a perk.

The office was hectic and telephones shrilled.
I did my work well, for I wanted to please,
And in typing and filing I was so skilled,
As my fingers raced over the typewriter keys.

Came the stampede for home, through all the long queues.
I'd flop in a chair with a biscuit and drink,
And would let my hair down and kick off my shoes.
When work was behind me I had time to think.

Why couldn't my life be peaceful and free?
I used to have hobbies and life was such fun.
I was buried in work, took no time to see,
The pleasures around me, nor let in the sun.

I gave up my job, then my car had to go.
I got a small puppy to take on my walk.
I took up my hobbies and learned how to sew.
My life was much slower, I had time to talk.

I strolled through the park with my dog by my side,
And saw how the sunshine broke through the trees,
How the rain fed the earth and the flowers opened wide.
Watched birds build their nests, and leaves dance in the breeze.

Simple pleasures of life now satisfy me,
I'm closer to nature, my soul is set free.
Life's a canvas - I paint the picture for me.
Back to basics has brought a new World to me.

S Maureen St. Clair

SIGN OF THE TIMES

While walking in the park today
I saw the children at their play
Up the steps and down the slide
Then on the roundabout to ride
With laughter and with cries of glee
The brave ones tried to climb a tree
While those more timid chased a ball
And kicked it up against the wall
The swings were full. Each little one
Determined not to miss the fun
Merrily swinging to and fro
Happy faces all aglow
Nearby the mums kept watch for danger
Scrutinising every stranger
I sigh and think of long ago
When we, as kids, were safe to go
Out to play, all on our own
Danger then was quite unknown
No one tried to harm us then
In those days of 'way back when'
I wish that it was still the same
It really is an awful shame
That children can't be left to play
Without their mums to watch all day.

Elizabeth Cook

MILORD'S PRAYER

What an excellent suggestion! Quite spiffing, don't you know.
The obvious direction in which Britain ought to go.
In recent years, the common man has got above himself.
He now believes the Marxist plan. To share a common wealth.

It's time they saw their betters curtail such anarchy,
and get right back to basics. It sounds top-hole, to me.
Let's hear small boys up chimneys, sing songs by Lionel Bart.
(A chap to clean my Bentley, would be a *super* start.)
A little man, who comes and does odd jobs around the place;
A pretty maid to dust my guns, in black skirt trimmed with lace;
A fat, but friendly woman, who toils below the stairs,
on kedgeree and partridge eggs; a stable-lad, who swears.

A miserable gamekeeper, to stalk the grounds and night,
and stop the peasants eating the game that's mine, by right.
In charge, a pompous butler, their duties to allot.
And *all* for bed and board. They would be happy with their lot.

But sadly, in the real world, it isn't like that now.
I had to sell the Bentley for less than seven thou.
The only thing that keeps me going; my reason to exist;
is sometimes when a lion escapes and *eats* a Socialist.

Lawrence Stewart

BACK TO BASICS

'Back to Basics', politicians say
Is their new slogan of the day
What does it mean in terms of life?
I think to be an old-fashioned wife
To work so hard throughout the day
And always feel too tired to play
And know tomorrow there's always more
Of what you've already done before
And ever more tax and VAT and bills
The pressure's on, it almost kills
We're going back, but it's not best
The past is dead, just let it rest.

'Back to Basics' means to me
A return to housewife drudgery
Of hands immersed in water, soap
Of constant cleaning, I can't cope
No vacuum, washer or microwave
No time spare, I can't save
And finally, this is no joke,
My lovely car, it has just broke!
Concetta Crawford

KEEPING THE FLAG FLYING

Although there's many super stores
Within our bustling town.
The shop that always comes to mind
Never lets you down.
For friendliness, and a daily chat
And service with a smile
Covers most things that you need each day
With quality, and style.
It's the corner shop, I'm shouting about
As my Mother did before,
When she used to save her coupons
During the Second World War.
Oh - it was a struggle, that's a fact
She saved old ones, months on end
Then she'd use them all at once,
And have a mighty spend.
Of course I'm talking of the days
When for just one and six
You could buy a loaf, half a pound of tea
And a nice selection of 'Bix'.
Mother often told me to keep the change
I would buy 2 ounce of gums
A weekly bonus I enjoyed
For my shopping trip for Mum.
And though the years have scurried on
My Mother was never skittish
Her words will always stay with me
'Don't forget Lad' she'd say
'Buy British'.

Ron Marriott